THE
EXERCISE
OF THE
PRIMACY

THE
EXERCISE
OF THE
PRIMACY

CONTINUING
THE DIALOGUE

ESSAYS BY

JOHN R. QUINN	JOHN F. KANE
R. SCOTT APPLEBY	THOMAS P. RAUSCH, S.J.
ELIZABETH A. JOHNSON, C.S.J.	WENDY M. WRIGHT

EDITED BY
PHYLLIS ZAGANO AND
TERRENCE W. TILLEY

A Crossroad Herder Book
The Crossroad Publishing Company
New York

1998

The Crossroad Publishing Company
370 Lexington Avenue, New York, NY 10017

Printed in the United States of America

Library of Congress Cataloging-in-Publication Data

The exercise of the primacy: Continuing the dialogue / essays by John R. Quinn . . . [et al.] ; edited by Phyllis Zagano and Terrence W. Tilley
    p.   cm.
"A Crossroad Herder book."
Includes bibliographical references
ISBN 0-8245-1744-X (pbk).
    1. Popes--Primacy--Congresses. 2. Episcopacy--Congresses.
3. Catholic Church--Government--Congresses. I. Quinn, John R.
(John Raphael), 1929-   . II. Zagano, Phyllis. III. Tilley, Terrence W.
BX1805.C655 1998
262'.13--dc21   98-11888
                                        CIP

CONTENTS

Acknowledgments

No text comes to life on its own, and this has been a particularly collegial exercise of scholarship.

We are grateful to the Steering Committee of the Roman Catholic Studies Group of the American Academy of Religion for supporting this project from its inception to its completion. The good sense and good cheer of J. Matthew Ashley, University of Notre Dame; John F. Kane, Regis University, Denver; Joseph Kroger, St. Michael's College, Vermont; William F. McConville, O.F.M., Siena College; and Patricia O'Connell-Killen, Pacific Lutheran School of Theology have made our varied tasks as co-chairs of the Group both bearable and productive.

The Roman Catholic Studies Group Session of the 1997 Annual Meeting of the American Academy of Religion on the afternoon of November 22, 1997 in San Francisco, "Continuing the Dialogue: John R. Quinn and 'The Exercise of the Primacy,'" which drew over 150 Academy members, was a year in the making. We are grateful to the Academy, and to Barbara DeConcini, Executive Director, for their support of the very concept of doing what the Pope suggested we do in *Ut Unum Sint*: bring church leaders and their theologians together to discuss the problems he noted in that encyclical.

To Archbishop John R. Quinn, retired Archbishop of San Francisco, the church leader who was willing to risk such a discussion with scholars in public, and to the theologians who prepared for and participated in that discussion, R. Scott Appleby, Elizabeth A. Johnson, John F. Kane, Thomas P. Rausch, and Wendy M. Wright, we are indebted for the seriousness with which they approached the tasks at hand.

Throughout the preparation of this volume we have profited from the gracious professionalism of colleagues, students and staff of our respective universities, especially at Boston University: Julie George and Lenin Martell, teaching assistants; David Suiter, School of Theology public services librarian; James Gallagher, College of Communication librarian; and Robert E. Hudson, Director of Libraries; and at the University of Dayton: Prudence Hopkins, Elizabeth Mayer, Anthony J. Mominee, and Veronica Murphy, graduate assistants; Meredith Moore and Brenda Fox, department secretaries. In addition, the valuable and gracious summer assistance of the student workers, librarians, and staff of Marymount College, Tarrytown, especially student worker Tamika Davis and Virginia McKenna, R.S.H.M., Librarian, cannot be overlooked or underestimated.

We are grateful to our editor, James LeGrys of Crossroad/Herder, and his confreres for their cheerful attention to the details of this work, and for seeing it through its multiple administrative hurdles.

Our thanks go as well to our families and personal friends who formed a not-always-willing audience and cheering squad for us as we completed the task of editing this volume. It is with their assistance and guidance we are able to complete the work we have set out for ourselves while remaining sane enough to enjoy the wonderful lives we have been given.

The Editors

Introduction

In 1995, Pope John Paul II published an encyclical entitled *Ut Unum Sint*—That All May Be One—that is both a plea for Christian unity and an invitation to dialogue. Pope John Paul II wrote:

> Could not the real but imperfect communion existing between us persuade Church leaders and their theologians to engage with me in a patient and fraternal dialogue in which, leaving useless controversies behind, we could listen to one another, keeping before us only the will of Christ for his Church . . . ?"[1]

A point of fraction the Pope identified was the exercise of the primacy on the part of himself, the Bishop of Rome. The problem he identified is neither new nor easily solved. While the Pope was specifically referring to the Petrine office as it is seen by other Christian communions—the plea is for Christian unity—the arguments within the Catholic Church make that plea all the more poignant. Clearly, internal Catholic struggles, particularly relative to the understanding of the exercise of the primacy, affect ecumenical dialogue.

Almost from its inception, the Petrine ministry has nurtured the development of the church in two ways: as a center of communion and leadership, and as a developing jurisdictional or organizational structure.[2] From the former comes the notion of collegiality among

---

[1] Pope John Paul II, *Ut Unum Sint* (Vatican City: Libreria Editrice Vaticana, 1995) 107, §96. The encyclical was promulgated on May 25, 1995. It is also printed in *Origins* 24 (1995).

[2] For historical data we rely primarily on Patrick Granfield, *The Limits of the Papacy: Authority and Autonomy in the Church* (New York: Crossroad, 1987); idem, "Pope," *s.v.*, *New Dictionary of Theology*, ed. Joseph A. Komonchak, Mary

the pope and bishops. From the latter comes the notion of collaboration with the pope on the part of the bishops. The unending challenge to the church as a whole, and to the papacy in particular, has been to balance these two ecclesial realities.

Historians place the inception of the practice of papal primacy in the second century when the Roman See, the honored See of Peter and Paul, became recognized as the center of the communion of the church. For example, Klaus Schatz notes the deference shown in Ignatius of Antioch's letter to the Romans as compared with his attitude toward other churches. Ignatius did not admonish or teach Rome because Rome was "preeminent in love" and "taught others."[3] This example, which some authors take as the earliest recognition of the primacy, notes the precursors of the two views that remain in tension: communion ecclesiology and juridical ecclesiology.

Some scholars see the first claim to primacy as juridical. Scott T. Carroll has argued that the first clear claim to papal primacy is found in a late second century sermon against gambling in the pseudo-Cyprianic corpus.[4] In the fourth and fifth centuries, the Roman See made even greater claims to a primacy of jurisdiction, but they were not much accepted by some other churches, for example, North Africa and Constantinople. In the West, however, the papacy continued to develop a stronger jurisdiction (and consequent juridical ecclesiology) that was especially supported by the "False Decretals" of Isidore in the ninth century. The title "vicar of Christ" first became proper to the pope alone in the thirteenth century under Innocent III, and symbolized an even further solidification of jurisdictional authority in the Petrine office. The Council

---

Collins and Dermot A. Lane (Wilmington, Delaware: Michael Glazier, Inc., 1987) 779-781; and Klaus Schatz, *Papal Primacy: From Its Origins to the Present*, trans John A. Otto and Linda M. Maloney (Collegeville, Minnesota: Liturgical, 1996). Except for references regarding specific points or direct quotations, further citations will not be made.

[3] Schatz, *Papal Primacy*, 5-6.

[4] See Scott T. Carroll, "An Early Church Sermon Against Gambling (CPL 60)," *Second Century* 8/2 (Summer, 1991) 83-95. The dating and authorship of this sermon are debated. Carroll notes that Adolf Harnack attributed the sermon to Pope Victor (189-99 C.E.).

of Florence (1438-45), not universally recognized as ecumenical, strongly affirmed a papal primacy of jurisdiction against Eastern claims, but the Council of Trent was unable to resolve disputed questions on the papacy and hence offered no definitive teaching on the point.[5] The statement of the doctrine of the primacy by Vatican I (1869-70), in its dogmatic constitution *Pastor Aeternus*, reaffirmed jurisdictional authority in affirming the doctrine that the Pope has full and supreme power, and ordinary and immediate jurisdiction, over every church, every bishop, and every believer, and that his decisions as supreme judge are also not subject to review, even by an ecumenical council. In practice, as Patrick Granfield writes, there is an "almost total absence of any practical limits to the jurisdictional authority of the Pope and his relationship to the episcopate."[6]

In short, papal primacy evolved from an informal recognition of the See of Peter and Paul as the faithful center of communion to the current affirmation of papal power; that is, from the perception of Rome as the center of collegiality to the perception of Rome as the center of *auctoritas et potestas*, of all authority and power, in the church. This seeming evolution to imbalance is at the heart of much of the controversy concerning the primacy.

The Second Vatican Council (1962-65) affirmed that the bishop of Rome is both the unifying center of the college of bishops (a view that fits with "communion ecclesiology") and the free authority who can exercise his papal office alone (a view that fits with "juridical ecclesiology"). Although Pope Paul VI saw primacy and collegiality as intrinsically linked,[7] today there remain serious tensions in theory

---

[5] See Schatz, *Papal Primacy*, 128-29, regarding Trent.

[6] Granfield, *The Limits of the Papacy*, 41.

[7] The doctrine of collegiality developed at the Second Vatican Council was opposed by a minority on the grounds that it undermined papal primacy. In a fascinating article, Peter Hebblethwaite has explored Pope Paul VI's reaction to a challenge to collegiality. Hebblethwaite cited notes Paul VI made on the night of 22 September 1964 as the Dogmatic Constitution on the Church was being crafted and debated. The pope had been studying the matter intensely and was convinced that the doctrines were intrinsically linked and that preserving such linkage was necessary for both to be properly understood. Hebblethwaite

and practice between communal (collegial, ecclesial) and juridical (collaborative, political) understandings of the church and of the papacy.

It is this widely-recognized tension that this volume examines. Subsequent to the publication of *Ut Unum Sint*, Vatican Secretary of State Angelo Cardinal Sodano said, early in 1996, that John Paul II had "'taken note' of requests from other religious leaders to find a 'new form' of exercising the Petrine ministry that would be open to a 'new situation.'"[8] It is from within the "new situation" that this book has grown.

On June 29, 1996, the feast of Saints Peter and Paul, John R. Quinn, retired Archbishop of San Francisco, delivered a lecture on papal primacy and the call to Christian unity at Oxford University on the occasion of Campion Hall's centennial.[9] The lecture was almost immediately posted on the world wide web,[10] printed in *Commonweal* and *Origins*,[11] and translated into and published in many languages.[12] The widespread media attention it received prompted public and private discussion, and the detailed response of at least one American Cardinal.[13] Those engaged in the media

---

concluded that "Paul was convinced that the doctrine of collegiality of Vatican II did not undermine papal primacy." Peter Hebblethwaite, "A Private Note and What It Wrought," *America* 158/23 (18 June 1988) 600.

[8] "Revision of Papal Primacy Hinted," *Christian Century* 113/12 (10 April 1996) 392.

[9] Quinn entitled his manuscript "The Claims of the Primacy and the Costly Call to Unity: Lecture on the Occasion of the Centennial of Campion Hall, Oxford."

[10] See http://mercur.usao.edu/www/faculty/shaferi/quinn.html. The first version was apparently posted on 6 July 1996.

[11] John R. Quinn, "The Exercise of the Primacy: Facing the Cost of Christian Unity," *Commonweal* 123/13 (12 July 1996) 11-20; "Considering the Papacy," *Origins* 26/8 (18 July 1996) 119-27.

[12] In French: "Réflexions sur la papauté: conférence de Mgr John Quinn, *La Documentation Catholique* no. 2137 93/19 (3 November 1996) 930-41; in Spanish: "Consideraciones acerca del Papado," *Mensaje* (Santiago, Chile) 45/454 and 45/455 (November 1996) 33-39 and 45/455 (December 1996) 29-37. The lecture has also been translated into and published in Vietnamese, Italian, and Portuguese.

[13] John Cardinal O'Connor, "Reflections on Church Governance," *Catholic New York* (25 July 1996) 4-5; reprinted as "On the Oxford Lecture: Reflections on Church Governance," *Origins* 26/11 (29 August 1996) 171-75. The same issue of

debate prompted by the Oxford Lecture seemed to choose sides based on their own ecclesiologies.[14] For the most part, the division was between those who argued for collegiality and those who argued for collaboration in the exercise of the primacy, a distinction drawn in Archbishop Quinn's lecture.[15] A specific point of division was the role of the curia, especially as it can step between the pope and the ordinary of a diocese. While John Paul II considers the curia to be part of his governing office, others argue that it is the curia that weakens both the church's governance and communion.[16]

Archbishop Quinn's Oxford lecture has quite possibly brought about more, and more serious, comment on the exercise of the primacy than any other single entry into the dialogue occasioned by *Ut Unum Sint*. It is a strong and deliberate, wholly honest and respectful examination of the current state of the papacy as it affects the wonderful project of church in this century, especially relative to the church's ancient and present preference for collegiality (characteristic of a communion ecclesiology), and the papacy's present apparent default to a curia-bound top-down controlling power structure (characteristic of a juridical ecclesiology). In the Oxford Lecture, Quinn distinguishes between the "ecclesial" model and the "political" model of church governance.

In questions and answers Archbishop Quinn released at the time of the address, he reiterated his call for an ecumenical council to be held in connection with the new millenium in order to respond to the issues of the "new situation." He cites the following issues as needing deliberation:

Origins published responses by Bishop James McHugh of Camden, New Jersey, and Archbishop Rembert O. Weakland, O.S.B., of Milwaukee, Wisconsin.

[14] Gabriel Meyer, "Prelate Gives Old Debate Another Spin," *National Catholic Register* 72/32 (11 August 1996) 1, 10; Gerard O'Connell, *The Tablet* (6 July 1996) 886-87; Bishop Kenneth E. Untener, "How Bishops Talk," *America* 175/11 (19 October 1996) 9-15.

[15] See pages 6-7 below, for Quinn's discussion of this distinction.

[16] Pamela Schaeffer, "Cardinal Arns Says 'Pope gives his curia free rein' the Pope replies, 'You are mistaken. The curia is the Pope.'" *National Catholic Reporter* 11/123 (11 October 1996) 2.

[T]he role of women in the church and in society, the celibacy of the clergy, the reception of the sacraments by person who are divorced and have remarried outside the church, contraception, an effective collegiality of the bishops, the meaningful application of the principle of subsidiarity in the church, the inviolability of human life from conception to natural death, the responsible use of the resources of the earth and the just distribution of wealth, inculturation of the Gospel and inculturation of the liturgy of the church, appropriate freedom of theologians.[17]

He calls for the creation of an atmosphere in which bishops can openly discuss matters which deeply touch the whole church because, as he says, "collegiality which is restricted to secondary issues is an attenuated collegiality."[18]

In San Francisco on November 22, 1997, the Roman Catholic Studies Group of the American Academy of Religion hosted a dialogue between scholars and Archbishop Quinn on his Oxford lecture. This volume presents that dialogue.[19] We include herein Archbishop Quinn's Oxford lecture, the five scholars' responses and comments, Archbishop Quinn's response to the scholars, and our own final comments on both the topic and the project. The dialogue in San Francisco was characterized by friendly courtesy, mutual respect, and an honest effort to understand, explore, and find ways to resolve the issues raised by *Ut Unum Sint* and Archbishop Quinn's lecture. That Quinn was graciously willing to be (as far as we know) the first American Catholic bishop ever to participate in a dialogue with scholars on his own work at the annual meeting of

---

[17] "Archbishop Quinn Discusses His Lecture," *Origins* 26/8 (18 July 1996) 127-28.

[18] "Archbishop Quinn Discusses His Lecture," 128. In his lecture, Quinn also said, "In addition, a collegiality which consists largely in embracing decisions which have been made by higher authority is a very attenuated collegiality . . . " (see p. 15, below).

[19] The papers as published herein are not identical to those presented orally; due to time constraints, most of the papers presented here were summarized for oral presentation and minor clarifications introduced for this publication. Most of the papers also retain the flavor of their oral presentation; we have not sought to edit out these characteristics.

the Academy—given the occasionally strained relations between bishops and scholars—is in itself a remarkable occurrence. That Catholics are a minority among scholars in the American Academy of Religion underscores the serious ecumenical interest in *Ut Unum Sint* and in the Oxford Lecture.

Each of the Academy members who participated teaches at an historically Catholic institution of higher learning within the United States.

R. Scott Appleby, director of the Cushwa Center for the Study of American Catholicism and associate professor of history at the University of Notre Dame, brings the perspective of an historian of American Catholicism to the discussion. His insightful paper examines the present tensions with regard to papal primacy in light of the modernist-integralist divisions early in the present century. He provocatively raises the question of whether we are retracing that unhappy path yet again.

Elizabeth A. Johnson, C.S.J., Distinguished Professor of Theology at Fordham University, shines light from contemporary feminist theology on the issue of primacy. Her wise and witty paper shows the importance of critical and constructive feminist theology for reflecting on authority in the church. She asks that the successor of Peter listen to the successors of Mary Magdalene as a way of beginning to resolve the tension between "ecclesial" and "political" modes of exercising authority in and for the church.

John F. Kane, professor of theology at Regis University in Denver, places the current crisis of authority in the Catholic Church in the larger cultural crisis of authority. His thoughtful essay affirms Pope John Paul II's diagnosis of the crisis of authority, but seeks to find a prescription other than the Vatican's authoritarian, "hardline" approach. He calls for a renewal of the Catholic imagination of authority in which the Catholic "both/and" is central so as to develop a theology that hold *both* collegiality *and* primacy together, rather than a theology or practice that makes either collegiality or primacy the governing norm.

Thomas P. Rausch, S.J., professor and chair of the department of theological studies at Loyola Marymount University, explores some of the crucial practical questions of ecclesiology today and their relevance to the issues of primacy. His challenging paper explores the issues of needed structural reform raised by Quinn, especially the issue of how the principle of subsidiarity can be of practical use in the church. With a perspective somewhat different from those of Appleby or Kane, he also explores the possibility that, as important as resolving structural issues is, the real issues concerning evangelization and ecumenism will arise and be addressed in different locales.

Wendy M. Wright, professor of theology at Creighton University, brings the perspective of spirituality to the discussion. Her illuminating essay brings the resources from the tradition of spiritual discernment to the dialogue. She notes how the resurgence of interest in Christian spirituality has created a new ecumenical approach to spiritual practices. She suggests ways in which we can continue to understand answers to the key question around which the entire discussion revolves: "What is God's will for the church?"

Archbishop Quinn's final paper responds to the challenges and suggestions raised by the five scholars.

We are honored to be able to bring together these exciting and important perspectives on a key issue in contemporary ecclesiology. We hope that you will find their insights on understanding God's will for the church in its present situation as instructive as we have.

Phyllis Zagano and Terrence W. Tilley
New York and Dayton
January 25, 1998
Feast of the Conversion of St. Paul in the
Octave for Christian Unity

The Exercise of the Primacy and
The Costly Call to Unity*

Most Reverend John R. Quinn
Archdiocese of San Francisco

I acknowledge with profound gratitude the honor that has come to me through the invitation of Father Munitiz, Master of Campion Hall, to give this centennial lecture. It gives me the opportunity to express my great admiration for those splendid, storied Jesuits who, for a century now, have served the Church with such distinction at Campion Hall in the heart of Oxford.

But I must also say how deeply moving it is to me that this lecture takes place in Newman's Oxford which is hallowed by such poignant and treasured memories of his journey *ex umbris et imaginibus in veritatem*. I hear again the distant voices of eager students echoing over more than a century and a half their confident proclamation, *Credo in Newmanum*.

The Feast of Saints Peter and Paul, observed today, turns our thoughts to Rome. And this centennial, by a double title, brings us very naturally to considerations of the papacy. The patron of Campion Hall, Edmund Campion of the Society of Jesus, was put to death precisely because he would not repudiate the primacy of

---
*A Lecture given on the occasion of the Centennial of Campion Hall, Oxford, June 29, 1996. Archbishop Quinn was then Visiting Fellow at Campion Hall.

the Pope. In addition, the Society of Jesus traces its very foundation to its fourth vow linking it to the Pope. It is eminently fitting, then, that on this centennial we should take up a complex and challenging invitation issued recently by Pope John Paul II.

THE CHALLENGE OF JOHN PAUL II

In his 1995 Encyclical Letter, *Ut Unum Sint*, on ecumenism, Pope John Paul II has this to say about the papacy:

> [T]he Catholic Church's conviction that in the ministry of the Bishop of Rome she has preserved, in fidelity to the Apostolic Tradition and the faith of the Fathers, the visible sign and guarantor of unity, constitutes a difficulty for most other Christians, whose memory is marked by certain painful recollections. To the extent that we are responsible for these, I join my Predecessor, Paul VI, in asking forgiveness.[1]

The pope plainly admits that there have been painful things which have wounded unity among Christians, and that together with others, the popes must accept some responsibility for them. This frank admission and the request for forgiveness place the pope in the line of Peter, the penitent. A study of early Christian art reveals that, after Christ, one of the most frequent images found in the first centuries is the image of Peter, Peter weeping for his sins.[2] The pope here identifies himself with that Peter who acknowledges and weeps for his sins.

He then goes on to cite his remarks to the Patriarch of Constantinople:

> I insistently pray the Holy Spirit to shine his light upon us, enlightening all the Pastors and theologians of our Churches, that we may

---

[1] Pope John Paul II, *Ut Unum Sint* (Vatican City: Libreria Editrice Vaticana, 1995), 99, §88. The encyclical was promulgated on May 25, 1995.

[2] *Encyclopedia of the Early Church* (New York: Oxford University Press, 1990), *s.v.* "Peter, part V. Iconography," 677.

seek— together, of course—the forms in which this ministry (of Peter) may accomplish a service of love recognized by all concerned.[3]

Then the pope issues this challenge:

This is an immense task, which we cannot refuse and which I cannot carry out by myself. Could not the real but imperfect communion existing between us persuade Church leaders and their theologians to engage with me in a patient and fraternal dialogue in which, leaving useless controversies behind, we could listen to one another, keeping before us only the will of Christ for his church. . . ?[4]

The object of the dialogue as the pope describes it, is ". . . to find a way of exercising the primacy, which while in no way renouncing what is essential to its mission, is nonetheless open to a new situation."[5] Rooted in the scholarly work of historians and theologians, there are doctrinal and historical questions about the papacy which have been discussed in the official dialogues among the churches for some thirty years. But the pope here introduces a new and important question: the "forms" of the papal ministry, "a way of exercising the primacy . . . open to a new situation." Thus the pope distinguishes between the substance of the papal office— "what is essential to its mission"—and the style of the papal office—the historically conditioned forms in which it has been embodied.

The pope himself, in apostolic discernment, sees that there must be new forms of exercising the primacy as the Church approaches the threshold of a new millennium. He calls the Christian family to look at how the gift which is the papacy can become more credible and speak more effectively to the contemporary world.

Those, of course, who respond to the request of the pope, must bear in mind the paradoxical nature of the project they are undertaking. The Holy Father asks for public consideration of new forms in which the Petrine ministry can be embodied and exercised. But one can only advance the need for new forms if the past or current forms are evaluated as inadequate. To consider inadequacy seriously

---

[3] Pope John Paul II, 106-107, §95.
[4] Pope John Paul II, 107, §96.
[5] Pope John Paul II, 106-107, §95.

is to embark upon careful criticism. This obviously must be done if one is to give attentive and loyal response to the papal request. But that very response, which issues out of an obediential hearing, can be misread as carping negativity, a distancing of oneself from the Holy See. Exactly the opposite is true. The pope has asked us for an honest and serious critique. He has every right to expect that this call will be heard and that this response will be especially forthcoming from those who recognize and reverence the primacy of the Roman Pontiff—as the church searches out the will of God in the new millennium that is before us.

The "new situation" is shaped by the shattering of the Berlin Wall and the collapse of the Communist dictatorships, by the awakening of China and her movement into the political and economic world of the twentieth century, by the movement toward unification in Europe, by a new and spreading consciousness of the dignity of woman, by the arrival of an immense cultural diversity in the Church, by the insistent thirst for unity among Christians. This new situation is not only political, economic, cultural and techno-logical. It is marked as well by a new psychology. People think differently, react differently, have new aspirations, a new sense of what is possible, new hopes and dreams. In the church there is a new consciousness of the dignity conferred by Baptism and the responsi-bility for the mission of the church rooted in Baptism.

The "new situation" is also one in which the Church confronts great challenges. It is estimated that by the year 2000 there will be more than fifty million internally displaced persons and refugees in the world. The gap between the wealthy and the poor nations is growing. There is real danger that Africa may become a margin-alized continent. Large numbers of Catholics are turning to sects or non-Christian religions.

The "new situation" for the primacy is indeed comparable to the situation which confronted the primitive church when it abandoned the requirements of the Mosaic Law and embraced the mission to the gentiles. This action required immense courage, vision and sacrifice. It was an uncharted path, a major change. There were grave reasons for keeping the Mosaic Law, not least of which was the fact that Our Lord himself had observed it. Yet trusting in the

Holy Spirit, the Apostles made that momentous decision. There was intense and bitter opposition to it, so much so that some scholars believe that there is founded evidence to show that it was ultraconservative members of the Christian community at Rome, opposed to the changes Peter and Paul had introduced, who denounced them to the Roman authorities and brought about their arrest and execution.[6] Similarly today, there are strong divisions within the Church and accompanying pressures pulling in conflicting directions. The decisions required by the "new situation" will be exacting and costly.

The church and the papacy in particular have to respond to this "new situation" and Pope John Paul II courageously asks the question of how the primacy can be exercised in a way that is open to this great cosmic drama.

My experience as a bishop for some thirty years, as President of the American Episcopal Conference, as Pontifical Delegate for Religious Life in the United States and as a member of a Pontifical Commission to deal with problems in the Archdiocese of Seattle, has involved close and frequent interaction with the pope and with the offices of the Holy See. It is in light of this personal experience that I want to propose my response to the Pope's invitation to rethink with him the style and manner of exercising the papal ministry "open to a new situation." First I will deal with my personal experience of the papacy. Then I will take up the need for structural reform, followed by some reflections on the Roman curia. In light of this I will make some observations about collegiality and the teaching, sanctifying and governing office of bishops with specific reference to the principle of subsidiarity in the Church. Finally, I will touch on the fundamental imperative in the search for a new primacy in a new situation, the imperative of the will of God and its bearing on the search for unity.

MY PERSONAL EXPERIENCE OF THE PAPACY

When he appointed me as Pontifical Delegate for Religious Life in 1983, Pope John Paul told me that he had a very personal interest

---

[6] See Raymond E. Brown, *Antioch and Rome* (New York: Paulist Press, 1983), 124-125; 168-169.

in this issue and that he wanted me to report directly to him and to come to see him often. As a result I did visit Rome frequently and when I requested it I was received by the pope at once and given all the time I needed. During these visits I was quite frank with him about my own views and convictions and set down my proposals for action with precision and clarity. In no instance did the pope reject my proposals or impose any preordained mode of action on me. He himself frequently spoke of the work as an act of collegiality. I found the experience to be in fact a brotherly collaboration in which the pope entrusted responsibility to me and supported me in carrying it out even in the face of some opposition both in the curia and in the United States.

From 1987 to 1989, when I was a participant with two American cardinals on a papal Commission charged to resolve problems in the Archdiocese of Seattle, I had a similar experience. At times there were differing views between the officials of the Holy See and our Commission about what course to follow. Differing viewpoints were expressed forthrightly and with candor by all the participants in our meetings with the pope. The pope listened carefully to all sides of the issue, but, in the end, almost without exception, endorsed the position of the Commission.

These examples show that the pope thinks in collaborative terms and that his personal style is marked by openness to ask for help and a willingness to listen. Yet these are instances not so much of collegiality as they are of collaboration by bishops in a task undertaken by the pope at his initiative. But in *Ut Unum Sint* he specifically mentions collegiality:

> When the Catholic Church affirms that the office of the Bishop of Rome corresponds to the will of Christ, she does not separate this office from the mission entrusted to the whole body of Bishops, who are also "vicars and ambassadors of Christ." The Bishop of Rome is a member of the "College," and the Bishops are his brothers in the ministry. [7]

---

[7] Pope John Paul II, 106-107, § 95.

The unity of which the pope is the sign and the guarantor is first realized and expressed in his relationship with the College of Bishops. This collegial unity is the fundamental paradigm for all the other ways in which the pope is the sign and guarantor of unity. In other words, the style and "way of exercising the primacy" in relationship to the College of Bishops determines in a primordial way all the other moments of unity of which the pope is guarantor and sign. And so collaboration by bishops with the pope in a task he specifically entrusts to them is not the full measure of collegiality. "Collegiality" is predicated of the bishops precisely because—with the pope—they have from Christ a true responsibility for the whole church. Hence bishops by this fact have the responsibility from Christ to take initiative in bringing forward problems and possibilities for the mission of the church. Collegiality does not exist in its fullest sense if bishops are merely passive recipients of papal directives and initiatives. Bishops are not only *sub Petro*. They are also *cum Petro*.

MORAL VERSUS STRUCTURAL REFORM

To ask the question about new ways of exercising the primacy "open to a new situation" is to raise the issue of the reform of the papacy. Yves Congar, the distinguished theologian, named cardinal late in life, has pointed out the inadequacy of a purely "moral" reform by which I understand him to mean an attitudinal reform. He believes that any true and effective reform must touch structures. He goes on to observe the lesson of history that personal holiness of itself is not sufficient to bring about a change and that great holiness has existed in the very midst of situations that cried out for change.

But he comes to a fundamental and inescapable challenge when he raises the question of why reform-minded men and women of the Middle Ages in fact missed the rendezvous with opportunity. Why did so little happen when there was such a general thirst for reform? Among other things, he cites their penchant for focusing on this or that specific abuse such as concubinage, failure of canons to fulfill their obligations in singing the office in choir, the notorious failure of bishops to live in or even visit their dioceses.

Most of those who wanted reform, he said, were prisoners of the system, incapable of reforming the structures themselves through a recovery of the original vision, incapable of asking the new questions raised by a new situation. Reform meant to them simply putting the existing structures in order. The further, deeper, long-term questions were never asked.[8] Their vision stopped at the water's edge. The moment passed, and a wounded church suffered incomparable tragedy.

It is these deeper, more comprehensive issues in regard to the exercise of the primacy that must be raised in the search for unity: What does a realistic desire for unity demand in terms of changes in curial structure, policy, and procedures? What do the signs of the times, the desire for unity, the doctrine of episcopal collegiality, the cultural diversity of the church, the new technological age call for in curial reform and adaptation to what the pope calls "a new situation"? What does all this demand of the pope himself?

THE ROMAN CURIA AND THE SEARCH FOR UNITY

Pope Adrian VI sent the nuncio, Chieregati, to the Diet of Nuremburg in 1522. This is an excerpt from the instruction the pope gave to him:

> You are also to say that we frankly acknowledge that God permits this persecution of His Church on account of the sins of men, and especially of prelates and clergy. . . . Therefore, in our name, give promises that we shall use all diligence to reform before all things the Roman Curia. . . .[9]

Here Pope Adrian affirms something which was one of the main concerns of the reform Councils of Constance and Basel, a promi-

---

[8] Yves Congar, O.P., *Vraie et Fausse Réforme dans l'Église* (Paris: Éditions du Cerf, 1950) 125-207.

[9] Yves Congar, O.P., *Divided Christendom* (London: The Century Press, 1939) 277.

nent concern of the Council of Trent, Vatican Councils I and II, and which continues to be of critical importance today: the directive power of the Roman curia, and the curia's need of reform.

One week before the opening of the second session of the Second Vatican Council, in September 1963, Paul VI himself stated the importance for the Church of a true and ongoing reform of the Roman curia:

> We have to accept criticism with humility and reflection and admit what is justly pointed out.
>
> Rome has no need to be defensive, turning a deaf ear to observations which come from respected sources, still less, when those sources are friends and brothers.
>
> The call for modernization of juridical structures and a deepening of spiritual awareness does not meet with resistance from the center of the Church, the Roman Curia. Rather, the Curia is in the front ranks of that perennial reform of which the Church itself, as a human and earthly institution, stands in continual need.[10]

Two years later, the Second Vatican Council itself explicitly called for a reform of the curia in its Decree on the Pastoral Office of Bishops in the Church.[11]

The curial system was not created by Pope John Paul II. Though the curia existed in some form since the time of Gregory I in the sixth century, it goes back, as we know it, to Pope Sixtus V in 1588. And so if we are to search for new ways of exercising the papal ministry we must go beyond the personal style of the pope and consider the curial system itself. The question of new forms or new ways of exercising the primacy is not only personal. It is also systemic. The curia and the pope cannot be completely separated.

---

[10] Pope Paul VI, "Address to the Roman Curia," Sept. 21, 1963. *Acta Apostolicae Sedis* 55/14 (12 October 1963) 797.

[11] Second Vatican Council, *Decree on the Bishops' Pastoral Office in the Church*, Oct. 28, 1965, §9, §10: "The Fathers of this most sacred Council, however, strongly desire that these departments . . . be organized and better adapted to the needs of the times, and of various regions and rites. This task should give special thought to their number, name, competence, and particular method of procedure, as well as to the coordination of their activities."

It is self-evident that the pope could not fulfill his responsibilities of communion and communication with more than three thousand bishops and dioceses in a wide diversity of cultures and languages without the curia. At the same time it must be admitted that any reformulation or change the pope may personally decide to pursue can be retarded or diminished, even thwarted, by segments of the curia which may not agree with him or may have a different vision. It is a matter of record, for instance, that powerful segments of the curia strongly opposed the convocation of the Second Vatican Council.[12] Paul VI touched on this in his 1963 address to the curia telling the members of the curia that if there had been resistance and disagreement before, now was the time for the curia to give public witness to its solidarity with the pope and the aims of the Council.[13] The pope is necessarily dependent to some degree on his curia for the effectiveness of his relationship with the College of Bishops and of his ministry.

My personal experience over many years in dealing with the Roman curia has brought me to appreciate the great diversity of its makeup. I have met in the curia men and women of great intelligence, broad experience, great vision and exemplary holiness of life. Many members of the curia serve the Church with extraordinary unselfishness and devotion and with little thanks. The Church is the beneficiary of their dedicated service.

But it is to be expected that in a curia of some three thousand people working in an array of secretariats, congregations and tribunals, not all share these qualities to the same degree. Some are very narrow, with limited experience, especially pastoral experience. Pastoral experience can provide a hermeneutic for statutes and laws which stands between wanton disregard and blind, rigid application. Laws, conscientiously upheld, assume another, more real value when seen in terms of people with names and faces and histories and personal struggles. The understanding of human nature is a necessary condiment of wisdom.

---

[12] Giuseppe Alberigo and Joseph A. Komonchak, eds., *History of Vatican II*, Vol.1 (Maryknoll, NY: Orbis and Belgium: Peeters, 1995) 133-135.
[13] Pope Paul VI, 795-96.

Yet it must be honestly acknowledged that many Orthodox and other Christians are hesitant about full communion with the Holy See not so much because they see some doctrinal issues as unsolvable, not because of unfortunate and reprehensible historical events, but precisely because of the way issues are dealt with by the curia.[14] It must also be said that this is a concern all over the world. Recent events in Switzerland, Austria, Germany and France, in Brazil, Africa and the United States are only one indication of how widespread this concern is. The concern has to do with the appointment of bishops, the approval of documents such as *The Catechism of the Catholic Church*, the grave decline in the numbers of priests and the consequent decline in the availability of Mass for the people, the cognate issue of the celibacy of the clergy, the role of episcopal conferences, the role of women and the issue of the ordination of women. Two things are involved in these issues: the decision of the Holy See on a specific issue and the way in which these decisions are reached and implemented. For instance, are such decisions imposed without consultation with the episcopate and without appropriate dialogue? Are bishops appointed against an overwhelming objection of people and priests in a given diocese? Where the answer to these and other such questions is affirmative there are serious difficulties for Christian unity.

The importance of a major structural reform of the curia cannot be underestimated. After the internationalization effected by Paul VI and the rearrangement of some competencies, the reforms which have taken place since have been relatively minor and have been designed by members of the curia itself. The major change of outlook and structural reform which "the new situation" requires would ideally be the work of a broader constituency. A commission, for example, could be created with three presidents. One, a representative of an episcopal conference, one, a representative of the curia and the third, a lay person.

Under this three-member presidency, there could be a working commission which would include bishops, priests, religious and lay

---

[14] Yves Congar, O.P., *Église et Papauté* (Paris: Les Éditions du Cerf, 1994), 59-64; Emmanuel Ghikas, "*Comment 'redresser' les définitions du premier concile du Vatican, Part II, La Primauté de Juridiction,*" *Irenikon*, 68/2 (1995): 182-204.

persons. The commission should be given a time line of not more than three years and should have authority to consult experts in management, government, theology, canon law and other useful disciplines and professions. The pope and the episcopal conferences should be kept informed of the progress of the work. When it is completed and in a state which the pope indicates he could accept, the plan should be presented for a vote to the presidents of episcopal conferences in a meeting held for this purpose and finally presented to the pope for approval and implementation. At this time the pope in consultation with the episcopal conferences could create an implementation commission to oversee the carrying out of the restructuring and with the mandate to report to the pope periodically. The work of the commission should be public and its conclusions should be public.

THE CURIAL SYSTEM AND THE EPISCOPATE

A prominent theme in the Second Vatican Council and in the teaching of Pope John Paul II has been the participation of bishops in the threefold role of Christ as Priest, King and Prophet.[15] This role is also called the threefold role of sanctifying, governing and teaching. In the dialogue on the forms and way of exercising the primacy, there must, then, be an important place for dialogue about how the style and policies of the Papal curia affect both the Pope's ministry as head of the episcopal college, and the collegial ministry of the bishops in communion with him.

The doctrine of episcopal collegiality is firmly in possession in the Church, explicitly affirmed by the Second Vatican Council and frequently invoked by Pope John Paul II. In any realistic dialogue about the primacy, there has to be some consideration of how collegiality is lived, and how, not merely in theory, but in actual fact, the Papal curia—an administrative structure—relates to and fosters collegiality—a doctrine of faith.

The curia is the arm of the pope. But the curia always runs the real risk of seeing itself as a *tertium quid*. When this happens, in

---

[15] Second Vatican Council, *Dogmatic Constitution on the Church*, §21.

place of the dogmatic structure comprised of the pope and the rest of the episcopate, there emerges a new and threefold structure: the pope, the curia and the episcopate. This makes it possible for the curia to see itself as exercising oversight and authority over the College of Bishops, to see itself as subordinate to the pope but superior to the College of Bishops. To the degree that this is so, and is reflected in the policies and actions of the curia, it obscures and diminishes both the doctrine and the reality of episcopal collegiality.

Yet the Vatican Council points out explicitly that the curia is in the service of the bishops. "These [the departments of the Roman curia] therefore, perform their duties in his name and with his authority [i.e., the name and authority of the pope] for the good of the churches and in the service of the sacred pastors."[16] The same risk exists also in regard to papal nuncios who can easily assume too great a directive power in regard to the episcopate of a nation, weakening the authentic collegiality of that episcopate. Nuncios, of course, can also be a source of great strength to episcopates under duress, encouraging them and backing them up when they take public positions denouncing injustice or oppression in a nation. And nuncios can play an effective role of reconciliation in countries where an episcopate is divided.[17]

COLLEGIALITY AND THE TEACHING OFFICE

Some years ago the future cardinal, Joseph Ratzinger, wrote that what the Church needs is:

> . . . not adulators to extol the status quo, but men whose humility and obedience are no less than their passion for truth; men who brave every misunderstanding and attack as they bear witness; men who, in a word, love the Church more than ease and the unruffled course of their personal destiny.[18]

---

[16] Second Vatican Council, *Decree on the Bishops' Pastoral Office in the Church*, October 28, 1965, §9.

[17] Second Vatican Council, *Decree on the Bishops' Pastoral Office in the Church*, §10.

[18] Joseph Ratzinger, "Free Expression and Obedience in the Church," *The Church, Readings in Theology*, Albert La Pierre, Bernard Verkamp, Edward

It is in that spirit, and in the interest of the honest and fraternal dialogue requested by the pope, that I would like to bring up some specific instances that I believe illustrate how the "way of exercising the primacy," as well as the curial system, have an important bearing on any realistic hope for unity.

I begin with the first of the threefold offices of Christ in which the Bishops participate, the office of teaching. It is significant that it was Pope Pius IX, who defined the dogma of papal primacy and infallibility, who also vigorously upheld the public statement of the German Bishops that bishops are not mere legates of the pope.[19] This doctrine was more amply articulated in the Second Vatican Council.[20] Such a doctrine cannot be affirmed in theory and denied in practice. Yet there are practical instances which are tantamount to making bishops managers who only work under instructions rather than true witnesses of faith who teach—in communion with the pope—in the name of Christ.

There comes to mind, for instance, the English version of *The Catechism of the Catholic Church*. On the positive side, bishops from various parts of the world were involved in preparing the *Catechism* and did in fact complete their work. An English translation was prepared which was agreed on by the English-speaking task force charged with its preparation. But objections to the translation were raised. Because of these objections, the Congregation for the Doctrine of the Faith halted publication, rejected the proposed translation and called for a completely new translation. The majority of the active English-speaking cardinals of the world supported the original translation and vigorously opposed any new translation. Yet they were overruled.

This suggests that the English-speaking cardinals, and the bishops of English-speaking countries, were not competent as teachers of the faith to judge the appropriateness or accuracy of an ecclesiastical document in their own language. This is certainly a diminishment

---

Wetter, and John Zeitler, eds. (New York: P.J. Kenedy and Sons, 1964), 194-217.

[19] Heinrich Denzinger, *Declaratio Collectiva Episcoporum Germaniae*, February, 1875; Editio XXXVI (Barcinone: Herder, 1976) §3113 & 3115; Pius IX, Letter to the German Bishops, *Mirabilis illa constantia*, March 4, 1875, §3117.

[20] Second Vatican Council, *Dogmatic Constitution on the Church*, §27.

of what it means to say that bishops share in the teaching office of Christ, and a diminishment of true collegiality.

In addition, a collegiality which consists largely in embracing decisions which have been made by higher authority is a very attenuated collegiality and the question must be asked how such limited collegiality truly responds to the will of Christ and how it responds "to the new situation." For instance bishops and episcopal conferences feel that such grave questions as contraception, the ordination of women, general absolution, and the celibacy of the clergy are closed to discussion.

The pope is not just a member of the Episcopal College. He is member and head. No one who understands this denies the pope the right to teach on his own initiative as he judges it necessary or appropriate. Granting that he has such a right, the real issue is when and under what circumstances he should prudently exercise such a right. Often discussion of these questions in the Church becomes frustrated because when they are raised it is said that one does not have sufficient loyalty to the pope or that there is a defect in one's faith. But faith and loyalty are not at question. It is the question of prudence and appropriateness. Far from signaling a lack of loyalty or defect in faith, raising such questions respectfully and honestly is in reality an expression of both faith and loyalty.

In the last century, a number of persons in Rome, as well as Cardinal Manning and others in England, thought that John Henry Newman, who expressed clear and principled objection to the opportuneness of the definition of papal infallibility and who spoke in strong condemnatory tones about the methods used by the pro-definition group, was lacking in Catholic faith and disloyal to the pope. Yet today, Newman is under consideration for canonization as a saint of the Catholic Church. Newman himself distinguished between the truth of a dogmatic definition and the prudence of the pope in making it.[21] This example makes it clear that while great emphasis has been given to the doctrinal aspects of the exercise of the primacy, too little attention has been given to the place of prudence in the exercise of the primacy. The doctrinal questions do

---

[21] John R. Page, *What Will Dr. Newman Do?* (Collegeville, Minnesota: The Liturgical Press, 1994) 120, 129.

not exhaust the discussion of the primacy. There is a legitimate and necessary place also for discussion of what is prudent at a given time in history.

Since it is the constant teaching of the Church that bishops are judges and teachers of the faith,[22] it would be more in keeping with this truth of faith if bishops were seriously consulted, not only individually but also in episcopal conferences, before doctrinal declarations are issued or binding decisions are made of a disciplinary or liturgical nature. In this way there would be a true, active collegiality and not merely a passive collegiality. It is true that Peter is charged by Christ "to confirm" his brothers,[23] but the brothers also support Peter. When Peter says, "I am going fishing," the others say, "We are going with you."[24] Some commentators are of the opinion that in this passage, Peter, despondent over the discovery of the empty tomb and not yet having encountered the Risen Lord, was returning to his former way of life. The others go with him to support him in a difficult moment.[25]

The bishops, if routinely and widely consulted on doctrinal and other important pronouncements, could be a better support to the pope, could help in bringing to bear the mind of the whole church on a given issue and in formulating a teaching so that the pope would not have to bear the burden all alone. The evident participation of bishops in these major decisions would also dispose larger numbers of people to accept them more readily. In other words, even in doctrinal matters, there should be an effort to prepare and dispose people to accept teaching. The ancient canonical principle, "What touches everyone must be approved by everyone,"[26] bespeaks not only prudence but an understanding of human nature.

---

[22] Second Vatican Council, *Dogmatic Constitution on the Church*, §25.

[23] Luke 22:32.

[24] John 21:3.

[25] Raymond E. Brown, *The Gospel According to John XIII-XXI*, The Anchor Bible (London: Geoffrey Chapman, 1972), 1091.

[26] "*Quod autem omnes uti singulos tangit, ab omnibus approbari debet.*" *Code of Canon Law 1983* (Washington, DC: Canon Law Society of America, 1983), canon 119, §3; *Code of Canon Law 1917*, canon 101, I, §2; Yves Congar, O.P., *Église et Papauté*, 42-43.

Newman postulated consultation in doctrinal matters not only because of prudence but also because of charity. He says:

> We do not move at railroad pace in theological matters even in the 19th century. We must be patient, and that for two reasons:—first, in order to get at truth ourselves, and next in order to carry others with us.
>
> The Church moves as a whole; it is not a mere philosophy; it is a communion; it not only discovers, but it teaches; it is bound to consult for charity, as well as for faith. You must prepare men's minds for the doctrine . . . .[27]

The international Synod of Bishops is another exercise of the collegial teaching office of bishops. But the synod has not met the original expectations of its establishment. The synod was envisioned as being a way for the bishops of the world with the pope to deal with major issues touching the Church. At the present time, however, the topic of the synod is identified by a small commission of approximately fifteen cardinals and bishops, elected by the synod, who present their proposal to the pope. Ultimately the pope chooses the topic. An approach more expressive of episcopal collegiality would be to charge the presidents of episcopal conferences to get input from their national conferences and then to meet together and vote on three topics in order of priority. The topic receiving a majority of votes would be presented to the pope for confirmation and approval for the next synod.

Many bishops feel that issues which they would like to discuss responsibly cannot come up, such as those mentioned above, as well as others, such as divorce, remarriage, and the reception of the sacraments. I am not here taking a personal position on any of these issues. My point is simply to underline that issues of major concern in the Church are not really open to a free and collegial evaluation and discussion by bishops, whose office includes being judges in matters of faith. A free discussion is one in which loyalty to the

---

[27] John R. Page, *What Will Dr. Newman Do?* 109; quoting a letter of Newman to Ambrose De Lisle of 7 April 1870, *The Letters and Diaries of John Henry Newman* 31 Volumes edited by Stephen Dessain *et al* (Oxford: Clarendon Press and London: Thomas Nelson and Sons, 1973-77) 25:82.

pope and the orthodoxy of faith of those who discuss these issues is not called into question. In subtle ways and sometimes in very direct ways, the position of the curia on these issues is communicated to bishops at synods and intimidates them. In addition it is made clear that certain recommendations should not be made to the pope at the conclusion of a synod.

Responsible for unity, bishops do not want to create an appearance of rebellion and so, perplexed, they keep silence. The bishops also have great faith and a personal reverence for the pope and do not wish to embarrass him by the appearance of conflict.

The procedures of the synod are outdated and not conducive to collegiality in its fuller sense. They would, in fact, prove alien to many of those seeking unity who are used to parliamentary procedures and more free exchange and debate on issues. A new way of structuring and holding these synods could have a significant effect on the search for unity and the exercise of true collegiality.

It would make the synod more truly a collegial act if the synod had a deliberative vote and not merely a consultative one. And this, too, would be a greater incentive to unity and a more authentic embodiment of collegiality.

Reflecting on a way of exercising the papal ministry more suitable to the times, we need to recapture the importance of ecumenical councils in the life of the church. The Council of Constance in the fifteenth century decreed that there should be regularly scheduled Councils every ten years.[28] If that decree had been observed perhaps the history of the Reformation would have been different.

A council is a witness of the unity of the whole church, of the bishops with the pope and the pope with the bishops. It is a witness that amid the certainties of faith, still the church does not have all the answers ready-made, that she must struggle and search for the truth, as the primitive church struggled over the doctrinal and disciplinary issue of the Mosaic Law.

It is difficult in today's world perhaps to say how often councils should be held but given the gravity of the problems and opportunities which confront the church today, the rapidity of change, the

---

[28] Norman P. Tanner, S.J., editor, *Decrees of the Ecumenical Councils* (London: Sheed & Ward and Washington, DC: Georgetown University Press, 1990) 438.

availability and instant character of electronic communication, the facility of travel, and the great diversity of cultures, I believe it would greatly benefit both the unity and effectiveness of the church if a council were held to mark the beginning of the new millennium. It would be timely if such a council were to deliberate on how often councils should be held given "the new situation."

COLLEGIALITY AND THE SANCTIFYING OFFICE

The second of the three-fold offices is sanctifying.

A number of bishops in various parts of the world believe that general absolution has beneficial effects in some instances and desire to authorize this practice. Certainly there are some obvious points against general absolution. For example, since the penitent does not have the opportunity for spiritual and pastoral direction in this circumstance he can be left with a troubled conscience. But it would be a fitting work of collegiality if bishops themselves could face the various problems connected with general absolution in a full and free discussion of its doctrinal and pastoral aspects.

Inculturation of the liturgy is another source of tension in many episcopates. Here the fundamental question must be raised and discussed: the principle that the Roman Rite must serve as *the* Rite in the Latin Church. When this principle was adopted in the Second Vatican Council there was not yet the sufficient appreciation or consciousness of the great cultural diversity in the church. The Roman Rite with its hieratic, measured gravity greatly appeals to many people and rightly so. But there are other cultures which are not well-suited to this approach. Bishops as judges of the faith and as those who preside over the liturgy and prayer of their churches should have the opportunity in synod or council to address this question more openly and in light of their experience. Difference in culture is, however, not the only consideration. We have also to keep in mind that there is a basic, common humanity shared by all peoples and which recognizes the need for reverence, adoration, the acknowledgment of the transcendence of God. There is as well the need for some common signs and practices in the church which express her universality and communion.

Collegiality and the Office of Governing

The third office of Christ is governing. Here I would instance the policies regarding the appointment of bishops. The process, as we have it in the United States, begins when a given bishop presents names of candidates to be discussed at a meeting of the bishops of a particular region called a provincial meeting.

At the provincial meeting, the names and qualifications of candidates are discussed in strict confidence and a vote taken. The names, with accompanying information, are sent to the nuncio in Washington, who forwards the list and the assembled information to Rome to the Congregation for Bishops. The nuncio's judgment is generally thought to have the greatest weight, more than that of the local episcopate. The material is then presented to a meeting of some fifteen cardinals and a few bishops who are called "members" of the Congregation for Bishops. This body discusses the candidates and votes on them. They usually, but not always, endorse the candidates as proposed by the nuncio. When the voting is completed the cardinal prefect of the Congregation for Bishops brings the results to the pope and the pope personally makes the final selection.

It is not uncommon for bishops of a province to discover that no candidate they proposed has been accepted for approval. On the other hand it may happen that candidates whom bishops do not approve at all may be appointed. There have been instances of priests of religious orders being named bishops without the knowledge of their own provincial superior and of diocesan priests appointed bishops when their own bishop was not consulted. Under the existing policy, collegiality in the appointment of bishops consists largely in offering bishops an opportunity to make suggestions. But the real decisions are made at other levels: the nuncio, the Congregation of Bishops, the Secretariat of State.

There are, indeed, certain things to recommend the existing procedure. It distances the appointment of bishops from local factions and pressures. It prevents the development of pressure groups favoring one candidate and rejecting another. In some instances it also removes the possibility of the State becoming involved in the appointment of bishops. Yet honest, fraternal dialogue compels me to raise the question whether the time has not come to make some modifications in this procedure so that the local churches really have a significant and truly substantive role in the appointment of bishops. In light of the decrees of the Vatican Council itself, the participation of the local churches in this process cannot properly be confined merely to the participation of bishops but must include a meaningful and responsible role for priests, lay persons and religious.

Until roughly 1800, Rome's intervention in the appointment of bishops in dioceses outside the Papal States was rare. Until 1829, it was the policy of the Holy See to leave the appointment of bishops to the local church where possible. At the death of Pope Leo XII in 1829 there were 646 diocesan bishops in the Latin Church. Of this number, excluding those in the Papal States, only twenty-four were directly appointed by Rome.[29] The present practice, therefore, is fairly recent. It has historic foundations in the chaos created in Europe by the French Revolution and the fall of Napoleon, and by the withdrawal of the Italian government from the process of the appointment of bishops in Italy at the time of the unification. In default of any other responsible agent, Rome was suddenly confronted with the need to provide for hundreds of dioceses. But simply because a policy became necessary at a certain time due to historical circumstances does not mean that it is prudent to continue that policy in all future times. It is obviously not a practice required by the nature of the primacy but one which developed because of historical circumstances.

COLLEGIALITY AND SUBSIDIARITY

Clearly linked, then, with the doctrinal truth of collegiality is the principle of subsidiarity. John Mahoney, S.J. has made the point that the word "subsidiarity" derives from the Latin word *subsidium* which means "help" or "support."[30] Hence the principle of subsidi-

---

[29] Garrett Sweeney, *Bishops and Writers* (Wheathampstead, Hertfordshire, Great Britain: Anthony Clarke Books, 1977) 199-200; 207-231.

[30] John Mahoney, S.J., "Subsidiarity in the Church," *The Month* 21/11 (November, 1988).

arity means that a larger social body with more resources does not routinely absorb the role or functions of smaller and less powerful bodies. But it does help and support the smaller bodies to be able to fulfill their own role. This principle, enunciated first by Pope Pius XI 1931 in his encyclical *Quadragesimo Anno*, gained wider understanding in the Church through the encyclical of Pope John XXIII *Mater et Magistra*. These two encyclicals, however, speak of this principle in regard to secular society.

But in a little-cited address to newly named Cardinals in 1946, Pope Pius XII explicitly stated that the principle of subsidiarity applies also to the internal life of the Church. The pope says:

> Our Predecessor of happy memory, Pius XI, in his Encyclical on the social order *Quadragesimo Anno*, drew from this line of thought a practical conclusion and enunciated a principle of universal validity: what single individuals, using their own resources, can do of themselves, must not be removed and given to the community. This principle is equally valid for smaller and lesser communities in relationship to larger or more powerful communities. And the wise pope (i.e Pius XI) goes on to explain, "This is true because all social activity by its nature is subsidiary; it should serve as a support for the members of the social body and never destroy them or absorb them." These words are indeed illuminating. They apply to all levels of life in society as well as to the life of the Church, without prejudice to her hierarchical structure.[31]

And Pius XII goes on to say:

> The Church as she moves through history pursues without hesitation the providential path of the times. So profound is this sense, this vital law of continual adaptation, that some incapable of rising to such magnificent perspectives, dismiss it all as opportunism. But no, the universal vision of the Church has nothing to do with the narrowness of a sect or with a self-satisfied imperialism which is a prisoner of its own traditions.[32]

---

[31] *Acta Apostolicae Sedis* 38/5 (1946): 144-146.
[32] *Acta Apostolicae Sedis* 38/5 (1946): 144-146.

A careful study of this address shows that the idea of subsidiarity in the Church is not a mere secondary consideration or an afterthought. It is central to what the pope is saying. Important too is the fact that he contrasts subsidiarity in the Church with the centralization of the imperialistic societies of our time.[33]

Subsidiarity in the Church has been a continuing concern. A distinguished member of the curia, Archbishop Giovanni Benelli, while serving as Substitute Secretary of State, made this observation:

> The real, effective power of jurisdiction of the pope over the whole Church is one thing. But the centralization of power is another. The first is of divine law. The second is the result of human circumstances. The first has produced many good things. The second is an anomaly.[34]

This concern has been expressed now over a period of thirty years. The Synod of 1967 voted to apply subsidiarity in the revision of the Code of Canon Law. The Synod of 1969 voted in favor of applying it to episcopal conferences. And in the Preface to the 1983 Code of Canon Law, we read that one of the important principles which underlies the new law is "the principle of subsidiarity which must all the more be applied in the Church since the office of the bishops and their powers are of divine law."[35] Notice that the reason given for subsidiarity is not because it is a sign of the times but for dogmatic reasons.

In order to do justice to this declaration of Pius XII, to the Vatican Council and subsequent documents, not to mention the aspirations of Catholics and other Christians who hope for unity, many of the existing procedures and policies involved in the "way of exercising the primacy" as well as of the papal curia need to undergo a major and thorough revision. This should recognize the true authority given to bishops by Christ and proclaimed by both the First and

---

[33] Joseph A. Komonchak, "Subsidiarity in the Church: State of the Question," *The Nature and Future of Episcopal Conferences*, Herve Legrand, Julio Manzanares, and Antonio Garcia y Garcia, eds. (Washington, DC: Catholic University of America Press, 1988), 298-344.

[34] Quoted in Yves Congar, O.P., *Église et Papauté*, 28.

[35] *Codex Iuris Canonici* (Vatican City: Libreria Editrice Vaticana, 1983) *Praefatio* xxii, §5, Latin text.

Second Vatican Councils and the popes who presided over them. Large segments of the Catholic Church as well as many Orthodox and other Christians do not believe that collegiality and subsidiarity are being practiced in the Catholic Church in a sufficiently meaningful way. The seriousness of our obligation to seek Christian unity sincerely, means that this obstacle to unity cannot be overlooked or dismissed as if it were the quirk of malcontents or the scheme of those who want to undermine the papacy. On more than one occasion, Pope John Paul II has said, "We must take every care to meet the legitimate desires and expectations of our Christian brethren, coming to know their way of thinking and their sensibilities."[36]

THE TWO PETERS

During a television interview I was once asked, "What is the strength of the Catholic Church?" The first thing I mentioned was the pope. The pope, because I was thinking about how the Second Vatican Council came about. The church and the world have some very grave and serious crises today. Both are going through a profound cultural shift. But the Catholic Church would be in an even greater and more chaotic condition if Pope John XXIII had not convoked the Vatican Council and given the Church a compass for this present turbulent age.

The Second Vatican Council is a witness of the importance of the pope for the existence and well-being of the church. Had there been no pope, the bishops of the world thirty years ago would never of themselves have come together, the priests of the world would not have called for a council and still less the lay people. But it was the vision of a pope with true authority who called the council. I think it very likely also that we would never have an encyclical such as *Ut Unum Sint* with its candor and openness if there had been no council.

Neither the sources of Revelation nor the facts of history present to us an idealized pope distanced from all human limitations and failings. Rather, the New Testament, theology and Christian art

---

[36] Pope John Paul II, *Ut Unum Sint* 97, §87.

present two portraits of Peter: Peter the Apostle, Peter, first among the Apostles; and Peter, the weak human being, Peter the penitent. While the ecumenical dialogues have tended to deal with the first, more doctrinal aspect of Peter, the second and human aspect should not be overlooked. When we speak of the human dimensions of the holder of the Petrine office we do not necessarily speak of moral failure as in the case of Peter who denied Christ. We speak of what it means inherently to be human, and that is to be limited. Even if we were to say that this or that pope was a perfect human being and a perfect Christian, he would still be a limited human being who could not know everything or please everyone.[37] The distinguished Scripture scholar Raymond Brown has observed that we never cease to be scandalized that the mystery of salvation has been placed in human hands.

In considering the papal office and the call to Christian unity, we have to confront the challenging truth that it is not permitted to defer unity until there is a pope who can fulfill everyone's expectations or agenda. We cannot hold unity hostage until there is a perfect pope in a perfect church. Christian unity will require sacrifice. But it cannot mean that all the sacrifices must be made by those who want full communion with the Catholic Church while the Catholic Church herself makes no significant sacrifices. Of the individual Christian the Scripture says, "You have been bought at a price."[38] Similarly, we all have to face the fact that unity among Christians will be bought at a price. All will have to sacrifice. If we are serious about the goal of unity, we must be serious about the cost of unity.

Gustavo Gutierrez was criticized by Rome for some of his work on liberation theology. When the media asked him his reaction he said, "I would rather walk with the Church than walk with my theology." He revealed his deep love for the Church even while suffering at her hands. Ignatius Loyola went to Rome with his first companions to offer themselves to the pope for whatever mission he might wish to give them. He could not see the pope just then because the pope, Paul III, was in Nice dealing with political affairs

---

[37] Pope John Paul II, 101-104, §91-93.
[38] I Corinthians 6:20.

and arranging the marriage of his grandson, Ottavio Farnese, to the daughter of the Holy Roman Emperor. Yet Ignatius and the first Fathers waited for the pope's return and then placed their talents, their future and their lives into his hands. They witnessed their faith and showed fidelity to the papacy in the face of the grave personal defects of the pope.[39] These are only a few instances in the long history of the Church of a wholehearted acceptance of and reverence in faith for the Church and for the person of the pope and his office.

And as our thoughts range over the specific examples I have raised today, it is clear that there is an underlying issue that needs to be dealt with. Pope Eugene III had been a monk under St. Bernard at Clairvaux. In the course of the lengthy letter he wrote to Eugene on his election, Bernard admonishes him, "You have been more the successor of Constantine than the successor of Peter."[40]

This admonition of St. Bernard was directed at the pomp and adornment of papal public appearances. While the Vatican Council has brought a greater simplicity to the modern papacy, and John Paul II has introduced further simplifications, Bernard's comment readily brings to mind the tension between the political model and the ecclesial model at work in the church. The fundamental concern of the political model is order and therefore control. The fundamental concern of the ecclesial model is communion and therefore discernment in faith of the diversity of the gifts and works of the Spirit. The claims of discernment and the claims of order must always coexist for one cannot be embraced and the other rejected. They must always exist in tension. But it is always wrong when the claims of discernment are all but eliminated in favor of the claims of order thereby making control and the political model the supreme good.

But in the end, the real question is not about the style or "forms" or the "way of exercising" the papal office, important and critical

---

[39] John W. O'Malley, S.J., *The First Jesuits* (Cambridge, MA: Harvard University Press, 1993) 71, 191; Andre Ravier, S.J., *Saint Ignatius Loyola and the Founding of the Society of Jesus* (San Francisco: Ignatius Press 1987) 29-35. Andre Ravier, S.J., *Les Chroniques Saint Ignace de Loyola* (Nouvelle Librarie de France, 1973) 40.

[40] St. Bernard, *De Consideratione* (Rome: Editiones Cistercienses, 1963) 453.

as these are. For in this encyclical on Christian unity, *Ut Unum Sint,* there is the unspoken question driving everything else. The ultimate question which the pope—and all of us who seek the unity of Christians—must ask first and last is: "What is the will of God?" The question we must address is in the last analysis not a question of management, it is not how to reconcile differences or resolve disputes. The question is: "What is God's will for Peter?" This is the courageous question Pope John Paul II has raised, the question he admits he struggles with and which he cannot answer alone.

Newman, who was treated very badly by bishops and by Rome over a period of many years, stands as an example of the search for God's will in the face of great personal suffering at the hands of the Church and the undeniable human defects of her ministers. When asked whether he had found what he hoped for in the Catholic Church, he replied:

> "Have I found," you ask of me, "in the Catholic Church, what I hoped and longed for?" . . . I did not hope or long for any "peace or satisfaction," as you express it, for any illumination or success. I did not hope or long for any thing except to do God's will . . . .[41]

The challenge of John Paul II to search out as brothers and sisters a new way of shaping the papacy as we approach the dawn of a new millennium is a sign of Christ, the Conqueror of sin and death and division. It is a sign of Him who is the Beginning and the end of all human history and who says, "Behold, I make all things new."[42] Christ as Lord makes everything new, a new heaven, a new earth, a new humanity. He is drawing us all forward into the future by the Spirit of the new covenant of love. We and the whole of creation are straining toward that future which God has prepared for those who love Him and do His will.

I am conscious that what I have said here today in Newman's Oxford has potential for distorted reporting and distorted appropriation by various extremes with their own agenda. These agendas are

---

[41] John R. Page, *What Will Dr. Newman Do,* 122; quoting a letter of Newman to Edward Husband of 17 July 1870, *The Letters and Diaries* 25:160-61.
[42] Revelation 21:5.

not mine. I speak completely in fidelity to the Church, One and Catholic. Indeed in the Second Vatican Council many cardinals and bishops said much of what I have said here today.

My reflections, then, are offered as a response to the pope by one who wishes to walk with him in an unbreakable communion of faith and love on the costly journey of discovery as together we search for the will of God. It is the response of one who reverences the papal office and the person of the pope, who loves the Church, who was born of her womb in Baptism, who received the name of Christ from her lips.

Most importantly, it is the response of one who prays to Christ each day as Newman did, " . . . that I may receive the gift of perseverance, and die, as I desire to live, in Thy faith, in Thy Church, in Thy service, and in Thy love."[43]

---

[43] John Henry Newman, *Meditations and Devotions* (Westminster, Maryland: Christian Classics Inc., 1975) 289-290.

Ending as It Began?
The American Century and the
Americanist Dream

R. Scott Appleby
University of Notre Dame

In the winter of 1909 John Ireland visited Rome for the last time in his life. The historian Marvin O'Connell relates the warm reception Archbishop Ireland and the party of Minnesotans accompanying him received from Pope Pius X. He also notes, however, that when Ireland preached at a mass held in the Church of San Silvestro, the "exceedingly prudent" rector of the North American College forbade his students to attend.[1] The archbishop's reputation as a progressive and sometimes "incautious" bishop remained firmly intact in Rome, if not in his homeland. At a subsequent meeting with officials of the Sacred Consistorial Congregation, Ireland was startled a second time when his orthodoxy was called into question. After the meeting, as he was making his way across the crowded Piazza Navona, Ireland turned to his assistant. "Do you know what they asked me?" he said in a quavering voice. "They asked me if I believe in the divinity of our Lord Jesus Christ!"

I was reminded of that anecdote as I read the text of Archbishop John R. Quinn's stirring lecture—all the more stirring because so

---

[1] Marvin O'Connell, *John Ireland and the American Catholic Church* (St. Paul: Minnesota Historical Society Press, 1988), 506.

moderate and reasonable in tone and substance. In particular, Archbishop Quinn's call for a discussion of papal primacy in which all parties are respected as speaking "in good faith," recalled similar pleas from priests and bishops in times past whose loyalty to the pope had been called into question by the curia. To the integralist mentality, one's ecclesiology and one's moral character are inseparable, and both are to be judged according to the unchanging mind of the Church. Unfortunately, the curia has repeatedly demonstrated a tendency to assume sole proprietary rights to the latter, a problem Archbishop Quinn identifies as persisting unto the present day.

The integralist habit of mind pervaded the Roman curia during the Americanist-Modernist crisis of the early twentieth century. To the curial officials who received him at the Vatican in 1909, the Archbishop of St. Paul's reputation as a leading Americanist had taken on darker implications in the aftermath of the condemnation of Modernism. In their understanding Americanism connoted the uncritical acceptance of religious liberty, church-state separation, and other principles associated with modern republicanism. The integralists believed that Americanists in France and the United States ultimately sought to bring the Church itself into conformity with the egalitarian principles and procedures of democracies. From their perspective, furthermore, a direct connection existed between the Americanist errors condemned by Leo XIII in 1895 *(Longinqua Oceani)* and 1899 *(Testem Benevolentiae),* and the heresy of Modernism, with its theories of vital immanence, historical evolution of the church, and premature endorsement of the Higher Criticism of the Bible.[2]

---

[2] In his 1899 letter to James Cardinal Gibbons, *Testem Benevolentiae,* Pope Leo XIII identified several errors of the so-called Americanists. In the spiritual realm, Americanism connoted a pronounced preference for the natural virtues and the active life over against the supernatural virtues infused by grace and the contemplative life. For a discussion of the papal encyclical on Americanism and the various interpretations given to it, see Thomas T. McAvoy, *The Great Crisis in American Catholic History* (Chicago: H. Regnery, 1957) and Philip J. Gleason, "The New Americanism in Catholic Historiography," *U.S. Catholic Historian* 11 (Summer 1993) 1-18. The entire issue is devoted to new perspectives on the Americanism crisis.

History remembers John Ireland as a colorful and innovative leader of the progressive party within the American hierarchy; as a champion of temperance, labor unions, and religious cooperation with public educators; and as a monarchical bishop who evinced unquestioning loyalty to the papacy and the hierarchical structure of the church. It is ludicrous to imagine him as anything other than a conscientious teacher and upholder of Roman Catholic orthodoxy and the doctrines of the faith. Curial officials nonetheless associated the Archbishop of St. Paul with the errors of Americanism and linked him to theological Modernists whose radical ideas he neither supported nor fully understood. Thus Ireland came to regret his casual support of the early researches of Alfred Loisy, the biblical scholar and French priest whose writings were later singled out for their heretical content.[3]

ENDURING PATTERNS OF CHURCH GOVERNANCE

Standard accounts of American Catholicism in the twentieth century place the "revolution" of Vatican II at the dramatic center of the story. They focus, accordingly, on change rather than continuity in Catholic thought, practice, and attitudes toward the world. In most respects, of course, this narrative structure is obvious as well as appropriate: the Council endorsed and capped radical shifts in Catholicism's ecclesiological self-understanding, and underscored its transformation from a European-centered to a truly global Church. The American church seemed to come into its own, its new status personified by the brilliant American Jesuit, Father John Courtney Murray, whose ideas on church-state separation and religious freedom formed the framework of the Council's pioneering Declaration on Religious Freedom.

---

[3] Ireland came into disrepute with curial officials for another, equally important, and related reason: the political fallout of the Spanish-American war, which some cardinals and bishops in Rome saw as an American exercise in anti-Catholicism. Although Ireland claimed sympathy with the Spanish side, he was identified with "Americanism"—a charge that he could not evade, especially after he apparently misreported to the Vatican a U.S. willingness to negotiate an early settlement to the conflict. See O'Connell's discussion of the episode, *John Ireland and the American Catholic Church*, 452-54.

If the topic is not religious freedom, liturgical reform, or the inculturation of the gospel, however, but the governance of the Church, the historian of twentieth century Catholicism might conclude that continuity rather than change is the appropriate theme. Archbishop Quinn's eloquent description of the unfulfilled promise of collegiality in the post-conciliar era—of papal consultation rather than collaboration, of curial indifference to the requirements of internal ecclesial subsidiarity—provides powerful support for this conclusion. In light of his remarks, one ponders the similarities between the Church of John Quinn's day and that of John Ireland's. Specifically, one asks: Despite the internationalization of the bureaucracy and the Council's unambiguous teaching on collegiality, has the enclave culture and integralist mentality of the Roman curia survived the twentieth century?

Certainly the milieu in which Ireland lived and worked was radically different from our own. For most of his career, for example, the American Catholic Church was considered a mission church and was under the direct jurisdiction of the Congregation for the Propagation of the Faith. The American hierarchy was much smaller in number, of course, and not fully "established," so to speak, either in American society or in the universal church. Moreover, the First Vatican Council supported an ultramontane reading of Catholic ecclesiology that the universal church did not significantly challenge until long after Ireland's death—until the advent of the Second Vatican Council. Despite these and other significant differences between the two historical periods, Archbishop Quinn's lecture points to the persistence of at least three patterns of institutional dysfunction:

1. A spirit of competition within the American hierarchy for the approval of the Vatican and the pope.

When Archbishop Ireland spoke publicly and boldly on controversial matters facing the Church at the turn of the century, several of his fellow American bishops—led by Michael Augustine Corrigan of New York and Bernard McQuaid of Rochester —protested to Rome and, at times, to the American press, that Ireland had misinterpreted or misread the clear teaching (or mind) of the Church on the matter in question. They also worked actively behind the scenes to undermine Ireland's standing with the Roman curia and the pope.[4] Meanwhile Vatican officials, although well aware of the tensions within the American hierarchy, acted neither to ease them nor to foster a spirit of reconciliation among the rival parties. To the contrary, curial officials, and the papal nuncio in particular, exploited the situation by playing one side off against the other. Ironically, the resulting perception of the American hierarchy as an unruly and contentious lot added weight to the argument in favor of the appointment of a papal nuncio with authority over national church affairs.

The debilitating consequence of this game of ecclesiastical politics is disturbingly familiar: a fractured and fractious faith community, some of whose clerical and lay leaders spent more time than was seemly arguing with one another and posturing for Rome while important pastoral issues awaited their undivided attention.

To this day the judgment of the nuncio carries more weight with Rome than that of the local episcopate, as Archbishop Quinn indicates in his discussion of the appointment of bishops (20-21).[5] And to this day the perception of rancor in the hierarchy perdures, especially where issues of American episcopal teaching authority vis-à-vis the Vatican are concerned. The range and intensity of individual bishops' public responses to Cardinal Bernardin's announcement of the Catholic Common Ground Initiative proved a recent case in point, as did the varied responses to Archbishop Quinn's Campion Hall lecture by some of his brother bishops.

---

[4] One thinks, for example, of the hostile reactions of Archbishop Corrigan and Bishop McQuaid to Ireland's announced support of the Faribault-Stillwater plan, by which the Archdiocese of St. Paul would enter into a partnership with the Minnesota public school system for the religious instruction of Catholic students. See Jay P. Dolan, *The American Catholic Experience: A History from Colonial Times to the Present* (Garden City, New York: Doubleday, 1985), 273-75.

[5] Parenthetical citations refer to pages in Archbishop Quinn's lecture in this volume.

2. Vatican discourse that lends itself to incompatible, contradictory and mutually exclusive interpretations (and to mutual denunciations, with each antagonist battering his or her opponent with quotes from pope, council, and consistory).

The official pronouncements, exhortations, rulings and teachings of modern Roman Catholicism have proved ambiguous, multivalent, and elastic—whether the topic was church-state relations, labor unions, or slavery in the nineteenth century; or liberation theology, free-market economies, or homosexual orientation in the twentieth.

In one sense the elasticity of the official discourse, if not of the doctrines it conveys, is a great strength of the Church. It regularly allows, and in a way invites, fruitful disagreements about the precise meaning and application of a Vatican directive or a papal encyclical.[6] The ambiguity of Vatican discourse can be a double-edged sword, however, producing division rather than complementarity. The rivalry between Archbishop John Ireland, seen as the most forceful and persuasive of the Americanists leading the progressive wing of the hierarchy, and Archbishop Michael A. Corrigan and Bishop Bernard McQuaid, the leaders of the Romanist or conservative wing, found expression in several specific issues (e.g., the school controversy, the status of Catholics who belonged to labor unions, the national character of the hierarchy, etc.), but at its foundation was a basic and mutually debilitating difference in how the two parties read and interpreted the mind of the Vatican.

By adopting an attitude of relative openness toward the pluralist society of the United States and its democratic culture, the progressives believed themselves to be following the example not only of their ideological leader, Isaac Hecker, but of Pope Leo XIII himself. In 1892 Archbishop Ireland supported the controversial appointment of a permanent apostolic delegate to the United States—over

---

[6] The standard example of the "fruitful ambiguity" of the papal encyclicals is the comparison of Dorothy Day and John Ryan, each formed by Pope Leo XIII's 1891 social encyclical, *Rerum Novarum* (The Condition of Labor), but developing its insights and principles in the American social context in two fundamentally incompatible but extraordinarily compelling, and Catholic, ways.

the objections of his friend and politically astute episcopal ally, James Cardinal Gibbons—on the mistaken assumption that "the policy to be followed out by the delegate will be fully along the lines of Americanism."[7] When Cardinal Satolli, the newly appointed apostolic delegate, turned against the Americanists as early as 1893, Ireland belatedly saw the wisdom of Gibbons' concern that the appointment of a permanent papal delegate might lead to a diminution of episcopal authority.

In accounting for the support Ireland and his friend, Rev. Denis O'Connell,[8] gave to the plan to appoint a permanent papal nuncio to the U.S., the historian Gerald P. Fogarty, S.J., points to the potentially misleading signals being sent by Vatican diplomacy at the time. *Au milieu des sollicitudes*, Leo XIII's call for the *ralliement* of French Catholics to the Third Republic, was promulgated on 16 February 1892, shortly after Ireland's arrival in Rome to discuss his plan to cooperate with the Minnesota public school system. Ireland and O'Connell received the pope's letter on the situation in France enthusiastically, and were further encouraged when a French newspaper quoted Leo XIII as extolling the United States as a republic where church and state lived in harmony and proclaiming that "What is fitting for the United States with all the more reason is fitting for republican France."[9] In this context, Vatican Secretary of State Cardinal Mariano Rampolla, who had crafted the pro-French policy, enlisted Ireland and O'Connell to support the plan to appoint a permanent papal nuncio to the U.S. The two Americans thus had every reason to see the appointment as a favorable development for their side. Yet, as Fogarty points out, the curia was not united on the policy of rapprochement between the Vatican and republican government. Cardinal Miecislaus Ledochowski, the newly elected Prefect of Propaganda, began to move curial policy

---

[7] Letter, Archbishop John Ireland to Austin Ford, St. Paul, September 23, 1892, Archives of the University of Notre Dame.

[8] Rector of the American College and "the Americanist agent in Rome" during the height of the Americanist controversy.

[9] *Petit Journal*, February 17, 1892, quoted in Gerald P. Fogarty, *The Vatican and the American Hierarchy from 1870 to 1965* (Collegeville, Minnesota: The Liturgical Press, 1982) 118.

toward Germany and Austria and away from France and America. *Testem Benevolentiae,* written toward the end of the aging pontiff's reign by his subordinates, was one result of the internal curial politics.[10]

This was not the last time that Ireland was led down the primrose path by Pope Leo XIII's Vatican, only to find himself advancing the wrong causes. In the 1890s he cited the pope repeatedly in various speeches and sermons calling for a new intellectual openness on the part of the American Church, and he reached out to Loisy in the same spirit. In the new century Archbishop Ireland discovered to his embarrassment and dismay that the Vatican discourse of intellectual openness had integrity only within a rigidly defined context in which Roman neo-scholasticism was seen as the exclusive framework for acceptable inquiry.[11]

In our own era the contested interpretation of papal and curial documents has become routine, with "liberal" and "conservative" camps forming around opposing visions of the Vatican II Church. Some outsiders to the Catholic community see this disputatious religious culture as a sign of intellectual health and spiritual maturity, while many insiders experience it as a painful and sad expres-

---

[10] Fogarty, *The Vatican and the American Hierarchy,* 119-22. The topic of mixed signals and "contested legacies" in the Americanist-Modernist conference is hardly exhausted by these few references. The meaning and status of Cardinal Newman's theological and ecclesiological writings, especially his essay on the development of doctrine, was one of the issues at the heart of the Modernist crisis. Many of the European priests implicated in the controversy, as well as their American supporters who published articles in the short-lived journal at Dunwoodie, *The New York Review,* invoked Newman as their inspiration and master.

[11] On this aspect of Archbishop Ireland's career, see the discussion in my *Church and Age Unite! The Modernist Crisis in American Catholicism* (Notre Dame, Indiana: University of Notre Dame Press, 1992), 80-1, 85, 87, 91. Progressive priests such as John Zahm, C.S.C. took seriously and acted upon the challenge issued by Archbishop Ireland and by John Lancaster Spalding, Bishop of Peoria, for Catholic scholars to engage in rigorous research, dialogue and public debate with Protestant and other Americans on a range of scientific and historical issues. When Zahm entered the public debate on Darwinian evolution and argued that Catholics were allowed to accept a theistic version of evolution, however, his work was censured by the Vatican.

sion of disunity, reflective of the culture wars raging in American society.

In any case, it plays havoc in the all-important realm of Catholic education and formation. Most of the church lives the faith outside the closed and self-referential circle of professional polemicists, pundits and academics. In order to do their jobs, however, catechists, campus ministers, DREs, and other ministers and educators charged with instructing and forming the faithful, seek clear exposition of the Church's social and doctrinal teaching. The bishops provide such statements in educational materials and diocesan newspapers, in pastoral letters, homilies and speeches (reproduced in *Origins*), and in several other fora. What some bishops have failed fully to absorb, however, is that the post-conciliar church is de-centered to an historically unprecedented degree. Catholics in the twentieth century have formed multiple associations, reinforced by multiple sites and sources of information, commentary and analysis. A simple example: millions of American Catholics relied primarily on secular newspaper accounts of Pope John Paul II's recent pilgrimage to the United States; some balanced these perspectives by listening to homilies or reading Catholic periodicals (themselves a mixed bag of opinions and reactions); fewer still relied exclusively or even primarily on "official" presentations of the substance and meaning of the papal visit.

The purveyors of the American Catholic version of culture wars take full advantage of these competing sites of religious (or quasi-religious) discourse to engender debate and discussion of a particular type. The presence of competing and uncoordinated sources of Catholic "teaching" is not a new phenomenon, of course, but mass media technology has changed the character of the discourse which emanates from these sources. That discourse is shaped more than ever by the exigencies and values of the media culture, in which information, fact, authoritative teaching, and opinion is ubiquitous, undifferentiated, presented without context and delivered at a pace hardly conducive to systematic reflection or analysis. In this milieu anyone seeking "clear exposition" of Catholic teaching requires sophisticated hermeneutical skills to determine the answer to basic questions such as: What is Pope John Paul II's position on democratic capitalism in general, and as practiced in the United States? What is the Church's official teaching on homosexuality? What is the Roman Catholic Church's attitude toward other Christian churches, toward Jews, toward Muslims, toward non-theists?

To each of these questions a variety of well-rehearsed and incompatible answers circulates in the American Catholic discursive community. Archbishop Quinn addresses a more difficult but no less basic question: What is the meaning of papal primacy in the church and the world today? How are Catholics to interpret *Ut Unum Sint*?

As we know, his answers have been publicly contested by other figures of authority in the American church and their polemicists, who claim that Archbishop Quinn misread the pope's invitation to dialogue on the question of the primacy.[12] While the public nature of the disagreement within the hierarchy on this and other matters is to some degree regrettable, it is preferable to the regime of secrecy and closed-door dealing that has characterized ecclesial culture, especially that of the Roman curia, throughout the century. The problem lies not in the existence of honest disagreement among the leaders and teachers of the church on complex and historically controverted questions which are open to several responsible interpretations, but in the lack of viable structures and procedures by which to discuss, clarify, and perhaps resolve such disagreements. In this regard Archbishop Quinn's call for reform of the synod by giving it a deliberative vote and not merely a consultative one, as well as his hope for a council to mark the beginning of the new millennium, seems particularly appropriate—indeed, urgent.

3. The Romanization of the American hierarchy as the Vatican's response to a major crisis in Catholic self-understanding and to the de-centering processes which ensued within the Church.

"Integrism in the American Church took place not through the repression of scholarship, which was virtually non-existent, but

---

[12] For example, see Rev. Richard John Neuhaus, "The Taming of the Church: Archbishop Quinn Speaks Up," *First Things* 67 (November 1996) 66-74 in which Neuhaus makes this criticism.

through the gradual Romanization of the American hierarchy."[13] Writing of the first quarter of the twentieth century, Fogarty documents the successful efforts of Cardinal Satolli and his successor as apostolic delegate to the U.S., Cardinal Sebastian Martinelli, to fill the American sees with ultramontane bishops. This was, Fogarty argues, the curia's most systematic and carefully considered response to the Americanist-Modernist crisis. The plan was to identify and appoint as bishops men who would leave the substantive theological formulations to the pope and the curia, while attending to the pastoral and institutional (i.e., brick and mortar) needs of their dioceses. The initial sign of the new order came with the appointment of William O'Connell as Bishop of Portland, Maine, in 1901. O'Connell was the first of a line of American bishops who depended on Roman rather than American patronage for advancement.

Romanization ensured the persistence of antimodernism at the highest levels of the American Church for decades, but it did not preclude the development of national episcopal structures and a national episcopal style. If the 1960s ushered in a revolution in many areas of Church life, the establishment of the National Conference of Catholic Bishops and its administrative arm, the U. S. Catholic Conference, provided the culminating moment in a long evolutionary process that began with the National Catholic War Council in 1917. Yet the NCCB also embodied the new spirit of reform, as did Pope Paul VI's internationalization of the curia and the appointment of Archbishop Jean Jadot as apostolic delegate to the U.S. Such developments seemed to confound the logic of Romanization, as did Vatican II itself, a pastoral council that called into question any formulaic or unnuanced approach to the task of translating the dogmatic and moral teachings of the magisterium into pastoral practice. The so-called Jadot bishops tended to encourage a measure of flexibility in this regard, an undeclared policy that both reinvigorated the pastoral life of the American Church and led to some abuses in the immediate aftermath of the Council.

Assessing the impact of Vatican II, Emile Poulat remarked that the Church had changed more in a decade than it had in the previ-

---

[13] Fogarty, *The Vatican and the American Hierarchy*, 195.

ous century: "The Church of Pius XII was closer to that of Pius IX than to that of Paul VI."[14] Once the dynamics of change were unleashed by the Council, writes the ecclesiologist Joseph Komonchak, "reform" established its own momentum, provoking conservative Catholics to complain of the decline in traditional popular devotions, the abandonment of distinctive clerical and religious dress, the political activism of clergy and religious, the exodus from the priesthood and religious life, the decline of Catholic professional associations, the spread of dissent and a pattern of confrontation with episcopal authority (particularly after the publication of Paul VI's encyclical, *Humanae Vitae*), and the movement for the ordination of women.

In the realm of ideas and Catholic self-understanding, change came most powerfully with the the collapse of the unitary neo-scholastic method and language of theology, and the introduction of genuine pluralism into American Catholic theology once Thomism was supplemented, and in many arenas supplanted, by narrative, feminist, liberationist and other inductive theologies grounded in experience.

Komonchak describes two broad schools of interpretation of the Council that have developed over the past thirty years.[15] The progressive interpretation characterizes the pre-conciliar Catholic Church as legalistic, hierarchical, patriarchal, parochial, and triumphalistic. The Council led the Church decisively into the modern world by retrieving apostolic models of worship, proclamation, and governance, and by restoring the spirit of true catholicity of the tradition in its outreach to other faith traditions, and to the poor and oppressed. The opposite interpretation of Vatican II makes use of a similar disjunction between pre- and post-conciliar Catholicism but reverses the judgments. The popes from Gregory XVI to Pius XII had rightly condemned the liberal modernity that was

---

[14] Quoted in Joseph Komonchak, "Interpreting the Council: Catholic Attitudes Toward Vatican II," in Mary Jo Weaver and R. Scott Appleby, *Being Right: Conservative Catholics in America* (Bloomington, Indiana: Indiana University Press, 1995) 17.

[15] The next few paragraphs follow closely Komonchak's chapter in *Being Right*, cited in note 14.

undermining Christ's reign over society and culture. The Church had effectively constructed itself as an anti-modern subculture with the tight organization and inspiring vision that an army of reconquest requires. All this was weakened if not destroyed by the Council, where the Church surrendered its distinctive vision of the world and its role in it. The consequences of this surrender to the secular world, the lament continues, are everywhere visible today.

These two interpretations differ not in describing what happened, but in evaluating what it meant and has come to mean. The first volume of a new history of Vatican II reminds us that the Council itself was not a peaceful event; it unfolded as a conflict between those who thought that relatively minor adjustments were sufficient and those who wished the Council to undertake a major rethinking of its redemptive role in the world.[16] It was a struggle between defenders of classical scholastic method and terminology, and those who thought that classical theology needed to be broadened and deepened by a "return to the sources" and by a renewed biblical and patristic orientation and expression. In terms of ecclesial structures, it was "a struggle between those who favored the highly centralized and uniform system that had developed in the previous century and those who envisaged a decentralization of authority that would enhance the role of bishops and encourage local adaptations and initiatives."[17] Throughout the Council the majority of bishops were "progressive," the minority (backed by the curia) "conservative."

When the conciliar reforms began to be implemented and, even more, when pastoral innovations began to reach beyond officially authorized changes, the conflicts played out at the Council itself continued. Liberals presented many of the changes, both official and unofficial, as implications of the Council, often by way of appeals and explanations that disparaged the pre-conciliar Catholic Church. By the early 1970s "the spirit of Vatican II" was being invoked to legitimate "reforms" that promised to go beyond the Council "for the sake of the Council." In at least one progressive American

---

[16] Giuseppe Alberigo, ed., *History of Vatican II, Vol I: Announcing and Preparing Vatican Council II Toward a New Era in Catholicism;* English version edited by Joseph A. Komonchak (Maryknoll, New York: Orbis, 1995).

[17] Komonchak, "Interpreting the Council," 22.

seminary professors told students that the requirement of priestly celibacy would be dropped, and women ordained for the priesthood "in the spirit of Vatican II."[18] Horrified conservatives responded to such developments in a variety of ways, not least by producing hundreds of treatises and books whose titles include words like crisis, decomposition, decay, and apostasy and appeal to metaphors like madness, betrayal, and desolation.[19]

All of this often makes it difficult to know precisely what is meant by the phrase "Vatican II," Komonchak concludes. In a narrow sense, the term refers to an event that occurred between 1962 and 1965 and to the sixteen documents it produced. A broader sense includes the officially approved reforms meant to implement it; a still wider sense includes also the unofficial reforms and the impact of both sets of changes on the church. Michael Novak speaks for many American Catholic conservatives when he writes:

> [T]he very meaning of Catholicism as a coherent people with a coherent vision has been threatened. . . . [The Second Vatican Council] set in motion both positive forces and forces that squandered the inheritance of the church. It set aside many proven methods and traditions. It fostered some experiments that have worked and some that decidedly have not.[20]

The conventional wisdom heard in liberal quarters of the American church for some years now is that the reign of Pope John Paul II and Cardinal Ratzinger has been characterized by a deliberate

---

[18] R. Scott Appleby, "Present to the People of God: The Transformation of the Roman Catholic Parish Priesthood," in Jay P. Dolan, R. Scott Appleby, Patricia Byrne, and Debra Campbell, editors, *Transforming Parish Ministry: The Changing Roles of Clergy, Laity and Women Religious* (New York: Crossroad, 1990).

[19] John Eppstein, *Has the Catholic Church Gone Mad?* (New Rochelle, New York: Arlington House, 1971); Dietrich Von Hildebrand, *Trojan Horse in the City of God* (Chicago: Franciscan Herald Press, 1967); Louis C. Bouyer, *The Decomposition of Catholicism* (Chicago: Franciscan Herald Press, 1969); Ralph Martin, *A Crisis of Truth: The Attack on Faith, Morality, and Mission in the Catholic Church* (Ann Arbor, Mich.: Servant Books, 1982); Anne Roche Muggeridge, *The Desolate City: Revolution in the Catholic Church* (San Francisco: Harper & Row, 1986).

[20] Michael Novak, *The Open Church: Vatican II, Act II* (New York: Macmillan, 1964).

policy of re-Romanization of the American hierarchy. On several occasions early in his pontificate the pope gave voice to his conviction that what the church needed most in an era of wrenching transformations in so many arenas was the stability that comes with a disciplined uniformity and obedience on the part of its clergy and religious who, in the familiar pre-conciliar formula, are "in the world but not of the world." Among the most impressive accomplishments of Pope John Paul II has been the success of his pontificate in reclaiming and restoring to centrality certain elements of pre-conciliar Catholicism briefly displaced during what one historian has called "the revolutionary moment" of Vatican II. Two prominent examples are the renewal of traditional piety, sparked by the pope's consistent support for conservative religious communities such as Opus Dei and reinforced by his own powerful example (e.g., his devotion to Mary); and a re-centering of the Catholic religious imagination upon Rome and the papacy itself, all the more striking because it has been accomplished amidst the equally telegenic and media-friendly globalization of the church and inculturation of the gospel. To his critics, however, John Paul II has also effected a far less benign reclamation—of the preconciliar dominance of Thomistic theological methods and schools. At times, it seems, the pope has attempted to stifle the vibrant theological pluralism that was the Council's greatest promise and that offered the most secure foundation for the kind of ecclesial reform called for by Archbishop Quinn and others. Yet theological pluralism continues to thrive in the academy, which has given Archbishop Quinn perhaps his most sympathetic hearing.

The re-Romanization thesis, to the extent that it is correct, situates Archbishop Quinn's 1996 call for reform in a particular context, one that helps to explain its reception in some quarters as being somewhat quixotic in character. Certainly the majority of bishops appointed by John Paul II are men unlikely to push the pastoral envelope or to tolerate non-traditional theologies. Even from within the hierarchy, a few particularly courageous Jadot bishops have complained not so much of the conservatism of the newer bishops (the term "integralism" has also been used), but of their mediocrity and lack of imagination as pastoral leaders. In turn the newer, conservative bishops have commented that liberals are too much taken with the so-called "spirit" of Vatican II and not sufficiently attentive to and bound by its actual letter.

In short, the occasion for the late twentieth century struggle over the governance of the Church is not the Americanist-Modernist crisis *per se*, but the meaning of the Second Vatican Council. Fundamental questions disputed in the earlier controversy nonetheless recur and remain unresolved at century's end: the status of the American hierarchy (and national structures) vis-à-vis the Vatican; the role of the papal nuncio and the curia in the selection of bishops and the overall governance of the American Church; the lack of effective structures for exercising collegiality or even sharing information, opinions, and ideas; the identification of progressive views on church governance, and the bishops who hold such views, with liberal or even modernist theological positions; and the smearing of such bishops' good names with the implication, subtly or openly advanced, that they transgress against orthodoxy.

As an extended footnote to this discussion, I close on a personal note addressed less to Archbishop Quinn than to his critics and detractors. To Catholic professionals of my generation (late Boomers) and younger, the ongoing debate over these questions seems increasingly irrelevant, and the principals almost scandalous in their self-absorption. The teachers among us are painfully aware that younger Catholics, victims of the postconciliar breakdown in effective catechesis and spiritual formation, hardly know what is meant by the term "Vatican II," much less "papal primacy." By "younger" I mean just about everyone under forty, not merely the college-age Catholics. The older generations of Catholic leaders—be they conservative, moderate, liberals, whatever—share an abiding faith in the church and its permanence and relevance to their lives. Their internecine feuding is bitter because so familial and familiar. But they *believe*. A younger generation, by contrast, is confronting a challenge far more radical than ever imagined by the "revolutionaries" of Vatican II. They are asking: Can we place faith in the existence of an objective moral order ?

In this light church politics as usual seems, as I say, scandalous. I mean this in no way as a criticism of Archbishop Quinn, for I recognize that the church cannot begin to respond to its most pressing pastoral challenges unless and until it brings its own house to order. Indeed, I introduce this concern not as an afterthought, but as another instance of the deleterious consequences of the persistence of gridlock on the fundamental questions addressed in Archbishop Quinn's lecture.

Going Fishing:
Papal Primacy and
The Words of Women

Elizabeth A. Johnson, C.S.J.
Fordham University

I would like to begin these remarks by thanking Archbishop John Quinn for delivering this Oxford address, an act of courage in the official climate of the Church at the present time. I would also like to congratulate him on the quality of the address. It is smart and insightful, with perfectly pitched rhetoric, well crafted argument, and effective use of both personal experience and intellectual sources. Two substantive points in particular stand out in my mind as excellent:

1) the understanding that episcopal ordination makes bishops not mere managers under the direction of the pope (the old "IBM model"), but genuine bearers of a shared apostolic mission from Christ in collegiality with the bishop of Rome, this view being not simply a response to the signs of the times but ancient, authentic doctrine; and

2) the consequent idea that in order to respect this charism of bishops and their pastoral concerns for the local churches, reform in the church needs to address not simply attitudes, but

structures, changing the way the current system of teaching, sanctifying, and governing operates through a huge curial bureaucracy.

John Quinn makes these fundamental ideas sing by lacing his theological and ecclesial insights with practical suggestions, thus presenting in one short package a wide-ranging proposal for reform. I wish we could clone him.

In this brief response, I would like to ponder the image of Peter presented in the Oxford address. At one point John Quinn tells a tale of two Peters, one the apostle, called to lead and strengthen the others, and the other the penitent, weeping over his denial of Jesus. These two images, Quinn points out, illuminate the fact that the holder of the Petrine office is in all cases a limited human being and may even be a moral failure. However, this should not block the road to the unity of the churches, for the validity of the Petrine ministry does not depend on the perfection of the human being exercising it.

In addition to the dialectic of these two images, there is also a third Peter in this address, brought forth to illustrate how bishops should be allowed to act as active rather than passive collaborators with the pope. Quinn argues:

> It is true that Peter is charged by Christ "to confirm" his brothers, but the brothers also support Peter. When Peter says, "I am going fishing," the others say, "We are going with you." Some commentators are of the opinion that in this passage Peter, despondent over the discovery of the empty tomb and not yet having encountered the Risen Lord, was returning to his former way of life. The others go with him to support him in a difficult moment.[1]

The problem with this reading is that whatever the sequence of later appearances of the risen Christ, all the gospels agree that the women disciples, led by Miriam of Magdala, discover the empty

---

[1] John R. Quinn, "The Exercise of the Primacy," 16 (above). Quinn's footnotes indicate that he is depending upon Raymond Brown's commentary on John for this idea.

tomb, receive the revelation of Christ's new life in the Spirit, and are commissioned to proclaim this good news to the male disciples, which they do. In fact, this Easter preaching by Mary Magdalene and the other women is but one moment in the overall gospel narrative of Jesus' death and resurrection in which the women form the moving point of continuity from death to burial to new life, and the point of connection between Jesus and the men, sequestered in fear and shame. Remove women's witness from these texts and the story falls apart. The announcement of resurrection by Magdalene and the other women thus has a special strength in light of the fact that they had looked upon Jesus' terrible dying and had performed the final mercies on his dead body. When they discover beyond tragedy a new coming of the Spirit of life, their commitment to spread the word is as profound as it is energetic.

Prior to Peter's going fishing in John's gospel, "Mary Magdalene went and announced to the disciples, 'I have seen the Lord'; and she told them that he had said these things to her."[2] Mark's gospel portrays the men's response in this way: "Now after he rose early on the first day of the week, he appeared first to Mary Magdalene, from whom he had cast out seven demons. She went out and told those who had been with him, while they were mourning and weeping. But when they heard that he was alive and had been seen by her, they would not believe it."[3] When Peter went fishing with the brothers, despondent over the future, his depressed state was not inevitable but was due to the fact that he had not believed the preaching of Mary Magdalene who bore witness to the Spirit's unimaginable new action in a world of violence and oppression.

In the second and third centuries, extra-biblical writings such as the "Dialogue of the Savior," the "Gospel of Philip," the "Gospel of Thomas," and the "Gospel of Mary" carry the trajectory of this tension between women's word and men's disbelief forward in accounts of rivalry between Peter and Mary Magdalene over her right to a leadership position in the community.[4] Consider the

---

[2] John 20:18.
[3] Mark 16:9-11.
[4] Texts appear in *New Testament Apocrypha* Vol. I and II, ed. Edgar Hennecke and Wilhelm Schneemelcher, trans. R. Wilson (Philadelphia: Westminster, 1963,

incident in the "Gospel of Mary," for example, where the male disciples, terrified by the death of Jesus, encourage Mary Magdalene to help them by relating what things the Lord has taught her. She teaches them assiduously until Peter interrupts in anger, asking, "Did he really speak privately with a woman and not openly to us? Are we to turn about and all listen to her? Did he prefer her to us?" Troubled at his disparagement of her witness and her faithful relationship to Christ, Mary responds, "My brother Peter, what do you think? Do you think that I thought this up myself in my heart, or that I am lying about the Savior?" At this point Levi breaks in to mediate the dispute, consigning Peter to the league of evil powers but defending Mary's role: "Peter, you have always been hot-tempered. Now I see you contending against the woman like the adversaries. But if the Savior made her worthy, who are you, indeed, to reject her? Surely the Lord knew her very well. That is why he loved her more than us." The result of this intervention is that the others agree to accept Mary Magdalene's teaching and, encouraged by her words, they themselves go out to preach.[5]

In an interpretation widely accepted in the academy, Elaine Pagels explains that such second and third century writings use the figure of Mary Magdalene as a symbol for women's initiative in ministry that was at this later time challenging patriarchal efforts, symbolized by Peter, to suppress female leadership in the developing "orthodox" ecclesial community.[6] We can but wonder how differently the history of the church would have turned out if, instead of going fishing, Peter in the early centuries had listened to the witness of women including Mary Magdalene, founding church mother and the "apostle to the apostles."

Obviously, I am reading John Quinn's address with the eyes of a feminist theologian, and I suggest that a feminist theological reading can extend and sharpen his analysis. For the heart of Quinn's

---

1966). For Mary Magdalene in the extra-biblical literature, see Karen King, "The Gospel of Mary Magdalene," in *Searching the Scriptures* Vol. II, ed. Elisabeth Schüssler Fiorenza (New York: Crossroad, 1994) 601-34.

[5] "Gospel of Mary," 17.18 - 18.15, Elaine Pagels, *The Gnostic Gospels* (New York: Random House, 1979) 77-78.

[6] Pagels, *The Gnostic Gospels*, 76-83.

proposal lies in the contrast he poses between two structures of church governance. One, the "ecclesial" model, thrives on communion and discernment and, in the case of bishops, shows itself in vital and active collegiality between the college of bishops and the bishop of Rome, which Quinn is advocating. The other, the "political" model, operates with an overriding concern for order and control, and results in the abuse of intrusive, top-down curial operations that Quinn decries. Both forms of governance have received broad and deep attention in women's theological scholarship.

EXTENDING THE ANALYSIS

While Quinn confines his analysis to papal primacy and the collegiality of bishops, tracing how the "political" model frustrates the effective exercise of episcopal ministry, I read his words with the wider picture of the whole church. I kept thinking: if he, an active archbishop, has felt so locked out, how much more the present governance of the Church has alienated so many of the rest of us, especially women. For we live in the historic moment when, due to the convergence of many forces, women are resisting inherited male definitions of female nature and roles that have consigned us exclusively to the private realm of nurturing and support. Instead, we are rediscovering our full human dignity as *imago Dei, imago Christi;* reclaiming the power of naming, both ourselves and the reality that human beings shape; and raising our voices in creative and critical ways to promote possibilities of being church in mutual and reciprocal relationships. Women are witnessing to the work of the Spirit in our midst in new and previously unthinkable ways; but Peter is still going fishing, accompanied by many of the brethren. In reaction to the rejection and the hurt, some women leave the church, some work to reform it; many are angry or annoyed in some way; myriads are now simply "defecting in place," Miriam Therese Winter's term for the maneuver by which women in the churches, both lay and ordained, forge ahead, claiming responsibility for their own spiritual lives despite the dictates of male power figures which are increasingly ignored.[7]

SHARPENING THE ANALYSIS

Arising out of this existential situation, feminist theology reflects on matters of faith from the perspective of women's experience and interpretation. In the categories of feminist analysis, Quinn's imperial "political" model of governance is at root nothing other than an expression of patriarchy, a form of social organization in which power is always in the hands of the dominant man or men, with others ranked below in a graded series of subordinate positions reaching down to the least powerful who form a large base. This pyramidal pattern of social relations in the church developed over the centuries in response to historical conditions, as Quinn notes. But it now rigorously maintains itself by appeals to divine will, thus depicting God as the Supreme Patriarch and tying the grace and truth of Jesus Christ to what has become a particularly authoritarian and obnoxious form of governance. Since by definition patriarchy excludes women, it is furthermore no accident that most of the examples of pastoral problems that Quinn cites have to do with women: the inclusive language translation of the *Catechism*, for example, which acknowledges the presence of women in the assembly; or the question of who makes a suitable candidate for ordination, whether a woman or someone married to one; or matters of sexual ethics, where women's bodies bear the burdens of the teaching; or the appointment of bishops who are pre-tested for their agreement on just such points. Tension arises because women are newly encountering the grace of the Spirit moving in their lives while church officials do not believe their testimony. Women know what they have experienced, however, and are not turning back. Consequently, before the rising tide of women's self-confidence in Christ leading them to seek an equal place in the assembly, ecclesial patriarchy is fighting for its life.

---

[7] Miriam Therese Winter, Adair Lummis, and Allison Stokes, *Defecting in Place* (New York: Crossroad, 1994).

In contrast to this patriarchal model, there are family resemblances, along with inevitable differences, between Quinn's collegial model and the vision of church described by feminist theology: a pluralistic church, in Anne Carr's words, that walks as an egalitarian, fully inclusive community of pilgrim people in solidarity with God and each other on their journey toward God's future;[8] a church in the round, in Letty Russell's depiction, with diverse charisms including various offices operating to encourage and support all as partners within a household of freedom;[9] a church that, to use Elisabeth Schüssler Fiorenza's inimitable phrasing, tries to cohere with that strand of the early Jesus movement that lived as a community of the discipleship of equals;[10] a church as humanity redeemed from sexism, as Rosemary Radford Ruether presents it, with Mary of Nazareth as the liberating symbol of all those who have been lifted up while the mighty are put down from their thrones.[11] In every instance the model calls for a mode of governance that respects the wisdom and commitment of the local *ecclesia*, gives voice to the insights of even its marginalized members, and galvanizes cooperation from the ground up rather than seeing the main function of bishops or church members as obeying or carrying out orders.

There is no inherent historical reason why bureaucratic patriarchy needs to shape the structure of the church, as examples from the New Testament make clear. Nor do theological reasons make this option a necessity. It is intriguing, for example, to see how Karl Rahner's vision of *The Shape of the Church to Come* depicts a declericalized church as a little flock that lives from its roots upward and is open, ecumenical, democratic and socio-critical all the while that it clings to concrete, gospel directives and grows in real spirituality

---

[8] Anne Carr, *Transforming Grace: Christian Tradition and Women's Experience* (San Francisco: Harper & Row, 1988).

[9] Letty Russell, *Household of Freedom* (Philadelphia: Westminster, 1987).

[10] Elisabeth Schüssler Fiorenza, *In Memory of Her: A Feminist Theological Reconstruction of Christian Origins* (New York: Crossroad, 1983).

[11] Rosemary Radford Ruether, *Sexism and God-Talk: Toward A Feminist Theology* (Boston: Beacon, 1983).

in a secular world.[12] Rahner even envisions that the pope could move on an annual basis, living for a year in Manila and then in New York City, etc., in order to be truly leader of the whole church, a mobility that would also deconstruct Roman bureaucratic centralization.

In the light of scripture and some theological tradition, therefore, Quinn's option for the "ecclesial" model in contrast to the "political" model can be upheld as legitimate and pastorally opportune. Even keeping the focus on pope and bishops alone, such a model can enable the ministry of bishops to be exercised in ways that genuinely lead and empower the local church and enable its members to become vital subjects of their own ecclesial history in a transformed community. As ecumenical dialogue over the role of Peter has shown, such a model can also facilitate a growing unity of the churches; for when the petrine ministry shows due regard for legitimate diversity, collegiality, subsidiarity, and Christian freedom, then it serves by functioning as the point of unity for the universal church and the church's voice of proclamation of the gospel before the world.[13]

CONCLUSION

The Second Vatican Council restored the biblical notion of the church as the whole people of God, called to the same holiness and sharing in the dignity and mission of Christ as prophet, priest, and king (*Lumen Gentium*), and committed together to the joys and hopes, the griefs and fears, of humanity on this earth (*Gaudium et Spes*). Since then, this "ecclesial" model of church has in fact been developing on the ground as together with men, lay and ordained, women have co-created ways of being church together that respect

---

[12] See Karl Rahner, *The Shape of the Church to Come*, trans. Edward Quinn (New York: Seabury, 1974).

[13] See Paul Empie and T. Austin Murphy, eds., *Papal Primacy and the Universal Church* [Lutherans and Catholics in Dialogue V] (Minneapolis: Augsburg, 1974); and Paul Empie, T. Austin Murphy, and Joseph Burgess, eds., *Teaching Authority and Infallibility in the Church* [Lutherans and Catholics in Dialogue VI] (Minneapolis: Augsburg, 1980).

the fundamental egalitarian character of baptism while honoring distinct charisms, all the while engaging in creative and challenging service of the world according to the call of the gospel. However, the tension between this vision of the church and the patriarchal, hierarchical model of the church whose adherents it calls to repentance and conversion is acute, even providing John Quinn with the occasion for his Oxford address. The profound contrast between the two models leads him to say in his own conclusion that the real question here is not about management style or ways of exercising the papal office. Rather, the ultimate question that faces the church is, "What is the will of God . . . ? What is God's will for Peter?"[14]

I would like respectfully to suggest an answer. God's will for Peter is that he stop going fishing and that for once, finally, he listen to Mary Magdalene.

---

[14] Quinn, "The Exercise of the Primacy," 27.

Roman Catholicism and the Contemporary Crisis of Authority

John F. Kane

Regis University, Denver

I have given my essay the title "Roman Catholicism and the Contemporary Crisis of Authority" since Archbishop Quinn's address is important not only for what it says directly about the exercise of papal primacy and episcopal collegiality, but also for what it thereby suggests about still larger questions of authority, secular as well as religious.[1] With this title I clearly assert that there is a major crisis of authority in contemporary society and culture, an idea that is certainly not original.[2] Yet I also want to suggest that Roman Catholicism might make many significant contributions in this civilizational crisis if it could begin to resolve some of its own internal crisis of leadership and authority. And Archbishop Quinn's

---

[1] In this short essay I can do little more than suggest the broad lines of an argument about such larger questions.

[2] The literature concerning the crisis of authority in modernity is vast. Two important writers are Canadian political philosopher George Grant and American sociologist Robert Bellah: See George Grant, *Technology and Empire* (Toronto: Anansi, 1969), *English Speaking Justice* (Toronto: Anansi, 1985), and *Technology and Justice* (Toronto: Anansi, 1986), Joan E. O'Donovan, *George Grant and the Twilight of Justice* (Toronto: University of Toronto Press, 1984), Robert Bellah, *The Broken Covenant* (New York: Seabury, 1975) and *Habits of the Heart*, written with co-authors Richard Madsen, William Sullivan, Ann Swidler, and Steven Tipton (Harper and Row: 1986).

important address indicates some of the ways in which this might happen.

I wish to argue (to put the essential points in a preliminary way) that the regime of John Paul II is largely right in seeing a growing relativism and skepticism, a loss of moral and religious authority, as one of the major problems in our world.[3] Yet the present papacy's way of responding to this problem does too little to help and much that may make the situation worse. Thus Archbishop Quinn's call for the reform of the papacy by a recovery and development of structures for real episcopal collegiality envisions a number of very important steps in the right direction. I also suspect, however, that his call for reform has at present little chance of getting a hearing in Rome, and thus little chance, at least in the short term, of making much difference for church or world. My own hopes for reform in the Catholic exercise of authority (and thus for a Catholic contribution to the wider crisis of authority), while they are nourished by the vision of hierarchical authority articulated by Archbishop Quinn, are finally based more on the possibility that key aspects of that vision are already being realized much closer to the ground in ordinary parochial and diocesan life.

THE IMPORT OF THE OXFORD LECTURE

Let me begin by stressing the importance of Archbishop Quinn's address. Perhaps I should simply say that it is one of those contemporary texts that deserves to be widely read and re-read as a source of hope and direction for contemporary Catholicism. It is, in other words, an authoritative text. It not only calls for renewal in the exercise of the collegial authority of the episcopacy, but is itself an important example of, or perhaps even a model for, the exercise of episcopal and collegial authority for the good of the universal

---

[3] This is a constant theme expressed not only in the Pope's speeches and encyclicals, but also in the practical agenda of his papacy, from the appointment of bishops and the orchestration of synods to the disciplining of theologians and attempts to "regain control" of seminaries and Catholic universities.

church.[4] And it speaks with authority not only because of the office of the speaker, but also because of the care and substance of its argument, the clarity and directness of its style, and the seriousness and pastoral concern evident in its tone. It is both carefully thought out and beautifully written.

As I read it, Archbishop Quinn's address develops around two fundamental and related ideas: his sense of the "new situation" (4)[5] within which ecclesial authority must operate, and the idea of "collegial unity" between pope and bishops as "the fundamental paradigm" which "determines in a primordial way" (7) the exercise of authority within the church.

In Archbishop Quinn's words, "[John Paul II] calls the Christian family to look at how the gift which is the papacy can *become more credible and speak more effectively to the contemporary world*"(3; emphasis added). In providing his own deft sketch of this "new situation," the Archbishop refers to momentous political "awakening" in Europe and Asia, to "new and spreading consciousness" among women and within diverse cultures, and to "a new psychology" in terms of which "people think differently, react differently, have new aspirations . . . hopes and dreams" (4). He goes on to speak of the "great challenges" of this new situation and refers to war and refugees, to the growing gap between rich and poor, and to the proliferation of sects. He does not refer explicitly to a "crisis of authority," but such a crisis is clearly implied in his references to awakening consciousness, a new psychology, the rise of sects, and in his later remarks about "this present turbulent age" where both church and world are "going through a profound cultural shift" and

---

[4] It is an ironic commentary on the situation of the Catholic Church that Archbishop Quinn had to wait until after his retirement to address the topic of the primacy and develop his suggestions for its reform. Perhaps it is true that reasons of pastoral prudence led the Archbishop to wait; or perhaps the time and occasion simply did not present themselves prior to the Pope's encyclical *Ut Unum Sint* (May 1995) and the Archbishop's subsequent sabbatical at Oxford. It remains nonetheless true (whatever the canonical subtleties regarding office and retirement) that this address is an important exercise of episcopal-collegial authority.

[5] Parenthetical references in this essay are citations to John R. Quinn, "The Exercise of the Primacy," earlier in this volume.

experiencing "very grave and serious crises" (24). New forms for the exercise of authority are clearly necessary in this new situation if, to repeat the Archbishop's words, the authority of the church is to "become more credible and speak more effectively to the contemporary world" (3).

In the search for such new forms of authority, Archbishop Quinn turns to his major theme: that the collegial relation of pope and bishops is "paradigmatic" for the exercise of authority in Catholicism within this new situation. In thus focusing on collegiality and, later in his address, on the correlative notion of "subsidiarity" (21-24), the Archbishop takes up one of the most fundamental contemporary issues concerning authority—the relation between higher or centralized authority and the decentralized (or participatory) forms of authority which stand under and, in principle, co-operate with, even as they have an appropriate independence from that higher authority. His talk deals specifically with the relation of papal primacy and episcopal collegiality, and thus with hierarchical authority within the Catholic Church. Yet it also deals, at least in principle, with authority in virtually every arena of church and society. For the relation of primacy and collegiality is, and not only for Catholics, a paradigm instance of the relationship of subsidiarity between higher and lower, or centralized and decentralized forms of authority.

Although the Archbishop refers explicitly to the idea of "subsidiarity" only toward the end of his address, the idea is present, as a principle governing the relation of different levels of community and authority, throughout his entire discussion of primacy and collegiality. To put the matter somewhat differently, the Archbishop argues throughout his address for an understanding of this relationship of higher and lower levels of authority in "both-and" or inclusive rather than "either-or," exclusive terms. If the church is to be both one and catholic, it requires *both* the strong, centralized primacy of papal authority *and* a strong, decentralized or collegial-episcopal authority. It needs both these levels of authority because, whatever the inevitable tensions and frictions of their ongoing operation, they nonetheless complement and mutually reinforce each other, at least in principle.

Yet what the church actually needs today, Quinn argues, is not just a reaffirmation in principle of this very Catholic vision of authority. As he says, "the doctrine of episcopal collegiality is firmly in possession in the Church" (12). And subsidiarity, as a principle which applies not only to secular society but "also to the internal life of the Church," has been clearly affirmed since the time of Pius XII and especially in the 1983 Code of Canon Law (22). What is affirmed in principle, however, has not yet been adequately realized in practice. As the Archbishop notes: "Large segments of the Catholic Church as well as many Orthodox and other Christians do not believe that collegiality and subsidiarity are being practiced in the Catholic Church in a sufficiently meaningful way" (24). What we need, then, is the recovery or the new development of *structures,* which will effectively realize subsidiarity by sustaining the tension, balance, and integration of primacy and collegiality as distinct forms of authority.[6]

Quinn's text, then, continually affirms the authority of the papacy as one of the major strengths and truths of Catholicism. Indeed it calls for reform of the structures of governance in the Catholic hierarchy precisely so that the papacy might be able to exercise its necessary authority effectively and authentically within the "new situation"—precisely, in other words, so that the papacy might be able to respond effectively and authentically to the many challenges (from relation to other churches and religions to the shortage of priests and the role of women to questions of sexual morality and sacramental discipline) which have arisen with such urgency in this new situation. And the text argues that the primary structural reforms that will thus strengthen the exercise of the primacy (and the exercise of authority throughout the Church) have to do with the recovery and development of forms of episcopal collegiality which Vatican II envisioned, but which have either been put on hold or actually reversed by the policies of the present papacy.

---

[6] See Archbishop Quinn's lecture, pp. 7-8 above, for his clearest statement of this need for *structural* reform.

Structures for Effective Collegiality

I agree strongly with Archbishop Quinn's call for this recovery and development of structures for effective collegiality. It seems not only doctrinally correct, but practically necessary for the recovery within the Church of an authority that is credible and effective. Quinn himself makes this point in his discussion of "the place of prudence in the exercise of the primacy" when he asserts that the "evident participation of bishops in . . . major decisions would also dispose larger numbers of people to accept them more readily" (16). It would, moreover, as he notes when speaking of the need for more frequent ecumenical councils, "witness that amid the certainties of faith, still the church does not have all the answers ready-made, that she must struggle and search for the truth, as the primitive church struggled. . ." (18).

It is precisely this witness that is so needed in our world today. One way to conceptualize the contemporary crisis of authority is to understand it as a series of different and conflicting responses to the situation which arises when new forms of consciousness and expectation, driven to urgency by the pace of economic and technical change, seem to have outstripped the ability of traditional institutions and authorities to provide adequate response and guidance. Thus many find themselves suspicious of or alienated from traditional institutions and authority structures, even as others cling desperately to them, and still others rush to embrace instant new authorities which have emerged in the vacuum created by the apparent inadequacy of traditional forms. The resulting situation (both in church and world) is one of growing polarization—between old and new forms of authority, and between all forms of institutional authority and a widespread retreat to privacy, with its emphasis on individual rights and freedoms. It is thus also a situation of heightened suspicion, distrust and contempt, a situation which not infrequently comes to expression in violence (whether in homes, on the streets of our cities, or in national and global conflict).[7]

---

[7] See Benjamin Barber, *Jihad vs. McWorld* (New York: Random House, 1995) for a contemporary geo-political discussion of the dynamics of this crisis of authority.

The very Catholic image of authority evoked by Archbishop Quinn not only stands in marked contrast to this situation of suspicion and polarization, but is a potential model for an alternative vision and practice of authority. It could, in other words, better enable the church to be that effective sign or sacrament of God's reign which it is called to be for our world. The church could provide an image of authority which is at once held by and faithful to traditional certainties, yet not having "all the answers ready-made" and thus having to "struggle and search for truth," an image of authority which is at once powerfully manifest in higher and centralized forms which nonetheless co-operate effectively with lower and decentralized authorities that have their proper separateness and autonomy. This complex and very Catholic image could be so significant and persuasive today as a response to the crisis of authority that characterizes our new situation. It was, for instance, no superficial accident of novelty or of "spin-doctoring" public relations that the four-year event of Vatican II provided such a powerful witness, which continues to evoke religious and political reverberations throughout our world. If the church is to become more fully such a sacrament, such an effective sign or image of God's graceful presence and merciful judgement—a sign of God's reign and authority—in our world, it will do so only by embodying more adequately in its own structures and life the kind of tension between fidelity and struggle, between higher and lower, one and many, which Quinn envisions in his call for structures that better integrate primacy and collegiality.

The specific reforms discussed in the Archbishop's address—a task force to reform the curia, a more deliberative voice for synods, and a council to mark the beginning of the new millenium—are all appropriate ways to begin to flesh out such a renewed and Catholic image of authority in the church. I do not have the experience or expertise that would allow me to make particular suggestions or

---

For an earlier, but far more subtle analysis of the growing climate of distrust and contempt, with particular emphasis on the significance of Christian faith in this situation, see William F. Lynch's *Images of Faith* (Notre Dame: University of Notre Dame Press, 1973).

criticisms regarding such specific reforms, but I find the most important reform which Archbishop Quinn discusses concerns the appointment of bishops (20-21). Without significant reform of this process, I think the entire discussion of primacy and collegiality remains, at least for the short term, fairly irrelevant. To put the matter very bluntly, a "pseudo-collegiality" exercised by a body of bishops who are essentially clones of the present curial mentality and purveyors of "party-line" thinking and discipline will do little to enhance the credibility and effectiveness of church authority.

Yet it seems—and perhaps I speak here with the ignorance of an outsider to the ways of clerical and ecclesial politics, as one whose sense of things is shaped too much by sensationalized media stories—that the Catholic Church is heading gradually, but relentlessly, towards just that kind of episcopacy, an episcopacy of men who see themselves as essentially vicars of the Pope rather than vicars of Christ (or as vicars of Christ only insofar as they are vicars of the Pope), of men who increasingly look very much like branch managers in a multinational corporation who serve the will of the CEO and his centralized administrative staff.[8] And it is this assessment which leads me to differ with Archbishop Quinn.

I do not think the reforms he is calling for have any chance of obtaining a real hearing, much less of actually being realized, given the present direction of thought and practice in Rome. This opinion may betray my ignorance of the actual complexity of realities in Rome and in various Bishops' conferences, or of the crosscurrents of thought and the ferment for reform within various clerical and theological elites, and may seriously underestimate the Holy Spirit. Yet Quinn's call for the recovery of an effective episcopal collegiality is, at least for the short term, directly and effectively contradicted

---

[8] There are perhaps some indications in Archbishop Quinn's text that he might at least partly agree with this assessment. See not only his critical discussion of the process for selecting bishops (20-21), but his earlier discussion of recent "practical instances which are tantamount to making bishops managers who work only under instructions" (14) and his concluding discussion of the "tension between the political model and the ecclesial model at work in the Church" (26).

by what one writer recently and accurately described as "the aggressive recentralization of authority under John Paul II."[9]

MODELS OF GOVERNANCE

Now many seriously critical things might be suspected and alleged about the present papacy and its "aggressive recentralization of authority": that it represents, regardless of its intentions, the *de facto* predominance of the "political model" over the "ecclesial model" in the governance of the church;[10] that it embodies the resentment of a declining clerical-aristocractic class before the ascendency of secular elites or the resistance of patriarchy to that rising feminist consciousness that it fears and fails to understand; that, by a tragic irony of contemporary history, it now expresses a fierce sacral will to power that was first forged in the fires of heroic resistance to the demonic will at work among the Nazis and in Stalinism.[11] Given the sinfulness of the human condition, it would only be surprising if there were no truth at all in such suspicions. Yet whatever their truth, it seems very important to note that the Pope's "aggressive recentralization of authority" *also*, and perhaps primarily, grows from a deep awareness of a pervasive climate of skepticism and relativism and a loss of moral and religious substance and authority in our world noted earlier, an awareness which I suspect is far more

---

[9] Charles R. Morris, *American Catholic* (New York: Random House, 1997) 333. For a similar assessment see Thomas Reese, S.J., "2001 and Beyond: Preparing the Church for the Next Millennium," *America* 176/21 (21-28 June 1997) 10-18.

[10] See p. 24 above for Archbishop Quinn's use of these terms. Historically, the accusation against the papacy for the predominance of power politics in Catholicism's structures of governance has been made in far more forceful terms by figures as significant as Luther (the "Babylonian Captivity"), Dostoevski (the "Grand Inquisitor"), and Simone Weil (the "Great Beast").

[11] A recent account of the 1997 Synod for America runs as follows: "One thing is clear. The pope is determined to keep control. . . . [He] is a man of incredible determination and will power. . . . His face is drawn and haggard. . . . But he struggles on. He remains always in charge." (Gary MacEoin, "Role of Synod...," *National Catholic Reporter* (12 December 1997) 12. Some might, perhaps, want to dismiss this characterization as typical "NCR journalism," but for the fact that the same emphasis on John Paul's strength of will is repeated frequently and favorably by many of the Pope's admirers.

clearheaded and accurate than that which prevails in many progressive or reformist circles in contemporary Catholicism.[12]

The Vatican's "aggressive recentralization of authority" is in large part its response to what it correctly sees as a deep and complex crisis of authority not only in the Catholic Church but in the "new situation" of our world. Its primary response to that crisis has been an insistent re-assertion of papal authority, indeed a growing extension of exclusively papal authority into more and more dimensions of Catholic life—if not a "creeping infallibilism," then certainly an even more pervasive "creeping papalism."[13] While the news image of a sternly vigorous young pope lecturing the world has been replaced by that of an aged man of suffering, driven to continue his journeys even as he clings to his processional crucifix for support, both images embody the same almost univocal and monolithic image of sacral authority. While that image is far too simplistic to convey the complex reality of the present papacy, it is still quite suggestive of the fundamental vision of authority expressed and developed in virtually every aspect of the doctrinal, disciplinary and administrative program of this papacy.

Yet this papal response to our pervasive crisis of authority is deeply flawed. Archbishop Quinn is correct in his for the most part implicit and indirect critique of the present papal program and the image of authority which it embodies—a critique that suggests that the present exercise of the primacy is less than fully credible and thus less than adequate to the needs of our times.[14] At times I find something almost tragic about the present papacy: its profound awareness of our civilizational crisis and yet the deep inadequacy of its response.[15]

---

[12] Considerable evidence and argument would be needed to provide adequate grounds for each aspect of this judgment, and for similar judgments expressed in what follows.

[13] For a key example of this extension of papal authority, see the account in Morris, *American Catholic*, 345-350, of the expansion of claims concerning the "ordinary universal magisterium."

[14] In saying this I am aware of Archbishop Quinn's caution that what he says might be "distorted" by people "with their own agendas" (28).

[15] Whereas some used the figure of Hamlet to describe Paul VI's later years, I am

One needs, of course, to be wary of premature judgments on what will undoubtedly be one of the longest and most influential papacies in Catholic history. Key aspects of its often controversial program have already proven very significant. It has, for instance, succeeded in slowing some of the centrifugal momentum emanating from Vatican II and in returning the question of Catholic substance and identity to the center of much Catholic consciousness. Yet it has not gained widespread acceptance for many of the particulars of its answer to that question, at least not in this country.[16] Rather its victories have been largely Pyrrhic. It has attempted to silence or discredit a few theologians while alienating many of the most active and committed Catholics. It has aroused an exaggerated hunger for certainty and righteousness in some narrowly "conservative" circles and among some of the young, while perhaps losing (or at least weakening) the loyalty of more than one generation of mainstream believers. For the most part, then, it has not only failed to successfully reassert its own authority, but has contributed in major ways to severe tensions and divisions in Catholic leadership circles and thus to a more general loss of authority within the Church.[17]

---

tempted to find in the present papacy something akin to Lear's tragically inadequate assertiveness.

[16] Empirical support for this and subsequent assertions about the effectiveness of the present papal program among American Catholics can be found in the summary of recent sociological studies presented by William D'Antonio, James Davidson, Dean Hoge, and Ruth Wallace in *Laity, American and Catholic: Transforming the Church* (Kansas City: Sheed and Ward, 1996). See also Andrew Greeley, "Polarized Catholics? Don't Believe Your Mail!" *America* 176/6 (22 February 1997) 11-15.

[17] While he cautions against the tendency to identify Catholic leadership with the papacy, Charles Morris, in the final section of *American Catholic* entitled "Crisis," places the blame for the critical situation in the American Catholic Church on the lack of a unified vision and strategy among Catholic leaders (320-321 and 429-431). Speaking of the crucial need for the Church to come to terms with "the pluralist ethic," with "the insistence on participation, the conviction that the *way* you get to an answer can be as important as the answer itself, the commitment to persuasion over diktat" (429), Morris offers the following as one of his final comments on the present papacy: "Even John Paul II, who, of all recent popes, has the breadth of vision and intellect to define a new dialectic between Catholicism and pluralism, is resorting more and more to command solutions, actively cutting off the discernment processes that are constantly working

It has also failed, in my view, to contribute significantly to re-solving the larger crisis of authority in contemporary society and culture. Here, too, of course, the picture is complex and it is certainly too early for definitive judgments. This papacy has clearly contributed to what might be seen as an almost global series of attempts to re-appropriate the sacred roots and dimensions of many aspects of personal and social life. And since this "post-modern" tendency is perhaps only at its beginning, it may well lead to a clearer and more assured recovery of the necessarily sacral grounding of all authority. Yet at present the picture is far from reassuring. Many efforts to re-sacralize authority involve reactionary fundamentalisms, which not only fail to respond to the new and very real challenges of our situation, but which further polarize that situation and thus contribute to the present crisis of authority rather than toward its resolution. And the present papacy's mostly univocal, top-down, "aggressive recentralization of authority," whatever its intentions, at very least risks contributing to this climate of fundamentalism and polarization.

Let me, at the risk of great oversimplification, give one example of the Vatican's failure to deal effectively with the wider cultural crisis of authority. It seems clear that the increasingly global movement to change the status of women and to rethink traditional understandings of gender necessarily involves a "shaking of the foundations" of traditional images and sensibilities regarding authority. For those deeply rooted traditional images and sensibilities have largely associated maleness with sacrality and authority in both domestic and public spheres. This, I take it, is a fundamental aspect of what is meant by patriarchy.

Now it is almost a cliche to say that the response of Catholic hierarchical authorities to the challenge of the present, global movement to re-understand and re-configure gender has been not only inadequate but deeply polarizing. Even many, like myself, who are quite sympathetic with the Vatican's effort (at recent U.N. conferences on population and gender, for instance) to combat a

throughout the Church." For a similar assessment see Thomas Reese, S.J., *Inside the Vatican* (Cambridge, Massachusetts: Harvard University Press, 1996) 275-278.

disintegrating overemphasis on individual rights in many liberal and feminist circles, or with its effort to evoke again a sense of the sacredness of maternity and paternity, find ourselves nonetheless dismayed by the way in which it has attempted to exercise its authority on issues related to gender. It has not only failed to operate collegially, to open a dialogue with the world's bishops (to say nothing of dialogue with theologians and the leadership of women's congregations and mainstream Catholic women's groups), but it seems to have actively frustrated efforts at dialogue by bishops around the world. It has operated by autocratic dictate (or given every appearance of doing so), thereby not only depriving itself of the wisdom and experience of so many thoughtful Catholic women who are deeply engaged with gender issues, but also contributing to the world's deep polarizations around such issues.

Of course, many of those espousing and benefitting from so-called "conservative values" are cheered by the Vatican's "hard-line" approach. Yet it strikes me that we Catholics are, as a result, not only much hindered in the inevitable task of working through the complex relations of gender, sacrality, and authority within Catholicism, but we have lost (or are very much at risk of losing) an historic opportunity to provide for the world the kind of image of moral and religious authority which Catholicism could and should be able to provide—the kind of image which was embodied by the highest levels of Catholicism at the time of Vatican II, the kind of image of authority called for in Archbishop Quinn's address.

CONCLUSIONS FOR THE FUTURE

Perhaps I have painted an unduly dark picture in response to Archbishop Quinn's hopeful vision of reform. Still, while I do not think that Archbishop Quinn's address will make much difference in the short term, I want to emphasize that we are nonetheless in his debt. It is important, especially at times like the present, that church leaders and scholars continue to remind us that the full truth of the Catholic understanding of authority must involve a very Catholic holding together of primacy and collegiality, of

centrality and decentralization, of unity and diversity. It is important that we continue to plan for the kinds of structures and practices that will make such holding together possible. It is important
that we continue to work, at whatever level, for the actual development and implementation of such structures and practices, and that
we recognize, affirm and support such structures where they have
already been put into practice.

To end on a more hopeful note, then, let me suggest that there
seems to be evidence that such structures and practices are actually
beginning to take firm root, not only in many religious congregations, but also in many parishes and dioceses.[18] Perhaps, then, the
development of a renewed, more adequate, and finally more Catholic image of authority is already underway—"from the ground
up," so to speak. Perhaps by a strangely ironic providence the
Vatican's present authoritarianism and its hard line on issues like
celibacy and women's ordination are actually contributing to such
renewal. For the priest shortage seems to have forced many dioceses and parishes into less clerical and more collegial forms of
leadership. And Rome's rejection of dialogue seems to have led
many committed Catholics, even as they maintain at least residual
loyalty to the person and symbol of the pope, to begin taking
much more initiative, no longer waiting for hierarchical direction
as they support and develop far more "collegial" and participatory
forms of authority.[19] While this tendency, especially in the U.S.,
runs the risk of creating sectarian fragmentation within Catholicism, at least in the short term it seems a necessary and healthy
response to papal intransigence. It may well be one of the things
which prepares the ground for the eventual achievement of the
kinds of hierarchical reform Archbishop Quinn envisions. That,
at any rate, is a hope to which I cling.

---

[18] See, for instance, the chapters on "Changes in Parish Life," "The Most-Com-
mitted American Catholics," and "Future Directions in American Catholicism"
in D'Antonio, *Laity, American and Catholic.*

[19] For instance, one could consider the continuing spread of the small Christian
community movement, and the rapid, even explosive, growth in Catholic (but not
hierarchically sanctioned) publications.

Archbishop Quinn's Challenge:
A Not Impossible Task

Thomas P. Rausch, S.J.
Loyola Marymount University

If the Roman Catholic Church is not a democracy, it is also true that it is not an absolute monarchy. Yet to many observers today, that is exactly what it has become. As Richard Costigan, a specialist on Vatican I, recently observed, the Catholic Church in the twentieth century "is a fully centralized church governed by a completely sovereign monarchical papacy."[1]

According to Catholic theology the church is not a single monolithic institution but a communion of churches, its authority is collegial rather than monarchical, and its hierarchical structure must respect the principle of subsidiarity which applies to the church just as it does to civil society. The ecclesiology of communion provides the sacramental foundation for the doctrine of collegiality[2] and has moved to the center of the Catholic Church's ecclesiological self-understanding as it seeks reconciliation with other churches and ecclesial communities.[3] If that reconciliation is to be realized, then the church must show that it honors collegiality and subsidiarity, not

---

[1] Richard F. Costigan, "Papal Supremacy: From Theory to Practice," *The Vital Nexus* 2 (September 1996) 9.

[2] Extraordinary Synod of Bishops, *The Final Report* C. 4; see *Origins* 15 (1985) 448.

[3] Extraordinary Synod of Bishops, *The Final Report*, C. 7; *Origins* 15 (1985) 449.

just in theory, but in its actual exercise of authority. Yet in his 1996 Oxford lecture, "The Exercise of the Primacy: Facing the Cost of Christian Unity," Archbishop John Quinn observed that "Large segments of the Catholic Church as well as many Orthodox and other Christians do not believe that collegiality and subsidiarity are being practiced in the Catholic Church in a sufficiently meaningful way" (24).[4]

In his address Quinn calls for a reform of the way that authority is exercised, a reform that touches structures, and he makes a number of specific suggestions. By way of response, I want to comment on some of those suggestions. But first, I would like to make some observations on the archbishop's interpretation of the "new situation" alluded to by Pope John Paul II in his encyclical *Ut Unum Sint*.[5]

THE NEW SITUATION

Like Pope John Paul II, Archbishop Quinn sees this "new situation" as offering an opportunity for entering into unity with other Christians. If Pope John XXIII made a distinction between the substance of the faith and its historical expression, he sees Pope John Paul II as making a similar distinction between the substance of the papal office and the historically conditioned forms in which it has been embodied (3). He points out that real ecumenical progress is not dependent on doctrinal agreement alone, but on a reform of the way that authority is exercised in the Catholic Church (11).

Quinn is right in emphasizing the importance of the reform of the church's style of government. But there remain substantial obstacles to reconciliation that go beyond questions of the exercise of authority. In spite of the emerging theological consensus on the nature of ordained ministry, the Catholic Church has not been able to move toward a recognition of ministry in the churches of the Reformation. Bishop Walter Kasper has suggested a way of moving forward, rethinking the doctrine of apostolic succession in terms

---

[4] Parenthetical citations refer to Archbishop Quinn's lecture, as printed earlier in this volume.

[5] John Paul II, *Ut Unum Sint*, § 95; *Origins* 24 (1995) 69.

of its being a sign of *communio* rather than seeing it in isolation as an unbroken chain of the laying on of hands, a mechanistic "pipe-line theory,"[6] beneath which lies the old argument of a uniquely transmitted sacramental power. Other theologians have developed similar arguments.[7] But I suspect the real obstacle inhibiting the Catholic Church's joining other churches in moving toward the reconciliation of ministries and sacramental sharing is to be found in the ordination of women. How can a church that does not accept the ordination of women enter into eucharistic communion with those that do?

Beyond being an opportunity for moving toward unity, Quinn sees some other dimensions to this new situation. He points out that it has been shaped by the political, economic, cultural, and techno-logical changes which have so marked the late twentieth century. But his interpretation does not end here. First, he calls attention to its psychological dimension: "People think differently, react differ-ently, have new aspirations, a new sense of what is possible, new hopes and dreams. In the church there is a new consciousness of the dignity conferred by baptism and the responsibility for the mission of the church rooted in baptism" (4).

Secondly, he compares this new situation for the primacy to that which the coming of the gentiles presented to the primitive church, a struggle which led ultimately to the abandoning of the Mosaic Law. At issue here for the archbishop is the question of how apos-tolic leadership deals with practical problems that call for change. For most of the first Christians, abandoning the observance of the Mosaic Law was unthinkable, for they saw the Law as mediating God's salvation and God as its author. Thus, what was required of the Christian community was a major shift in its self-understanding and way of living, from an emphasis on Abrahamic descent and observance of the Law to a new *koinonia* in Christ and justification by faith. But such a shift was not easy; Quinn notes that the bitter-

---

[6] Bishop Walter Kasper, "Apostolic Succession in Episcopacy in an Ecumenical Context," *The Bicentennial Lecture*, ed. Rudi Ruckmann (Baltimore, Maryland: St. Mary's Seminary and University, 1992) 8.

[7] Cf. David N. Power, "Roman Catholic Theologies of Eucharistic Communion: A Contribution to Ecumenical Conversation," *Theological Studies* 57 (1996) 609.

ness and division it occasioned may have brought about the death of the two founding apostles of the Roman church, Peter and Paul. So too, the decisions the new situation requires of the church today will be exacting and costly.

But if apostolic leadership is being called to acknowledge the need for change in the light of a new situation, another significant shift, characterized by a different way of thinking and acting and by a new understanding of how salvation is mediated, may already have taken place in the faithful.

In locales like the United States and western Europe, Catholics as much as any others have been influenced by the spirit of late modernity. That spirit is individualistic, subjective, and anti-institutional. The modern tendency to separate spirituality from institutional religion, so often commented on by social scientists and theologians, has weakened ecclesiastical authority in general. In *A Generation of Seekers*, Wade Clark Roof has emphasized the highly subjective approach to religion of the "baby boomers" who "value experience over beliefs, distrust institutions and leaders, stress personal fulfillment yet yearn for community, and are fluid in their allegiances."[8] Robert Wuthnow, in his study of small support groups, two-thirds of which have some connection to a church or synagogue, observes that in the adaptation of spirituality to modern social conditions "the sacred is being redefined, turned on its authoritarian head, made more populist, practical, and experiential."[9] Meredith McGuire describes the "spiritual autonomy" of many contemporary believers who "feel free to choose components of their individual faith and practice, combining elements of their official religious tradition with other culturally available elements."[10] Miriam Therese Winter writes about women influenced by feminism, both Catholic and mainline Protestant, who are "defecting in place," remaining within the religious community but developing

---

[8] Wade Clark Roof, *A Generation of Seekers: the Spiritual Journeys of the Baby Boomer Generation* (San Francisco: HarperCollins, 1993), 8.

[9] Robert Wuthnow, *Sharing the Journey: Support Groups and America's New Quest for Community* (New York: The Free Press, 1994), 360.

[10] Meredith B. McGuire, "Mapping Contemporary American Spirituality: A Sociological Perspective," *Christian Spirituality Bulletin* 5/1 (1997) 4.

alternative rituals and spiritual practices independent of and often not approved by church leadership.[11] What these studies show is that many "religious" people today show considerable independence from traditional religious authority. They regard experience as more important than doctrine or dogma, are spiritually eclectic, place a high value on group sharing and tolerance, and put personal fulfillment ahead of institutional loyalty.

The credibility of Roman Catholic magisterial authority in particular has suffered an enormous loss, beginning with Pope Paul VI's reaffirmation of the traditional ban on contraception in his 1967 encyclical *Humanae Vitae*.[12] The pope's teaching was difficult for many Catholics to accept, and doubt here quickly led to doubt elsewhere. The resulting loss of credibility means that the rationales given by church authority for its rules and policies no longer convince. Thomas J. Reese gives the example of trying to explain to a child why his mother cannot go to Communion because she is remarried without an annulment or belongs to another church; the child will think the church is saying that his mother is a bad person: "If millions of American Catholic children are forced to choose between loyalty to their church or to their parent, the church will lose."[13] People begin to make up their own minds.

Today an increasing number of Catholics quietly ignore the Church's rules on divorce and remarriage, its eucharistic discipline, its teaching in the areas of sexuality and social justice. They are often impatient with institutional concerns and want to be included in the formulation of doctrine. Roof reports that "An astounding 95%

[11] Miriam Therese Winter, Adair T. Lummis, and Allison Stokes, *Defecting in Place: Women Claiming Responsibility for Their Own Spiritual Lives* (New York: Crossroad, 1994).

[12] See George Gallup, Jr. and Jim Castelli, *The American Catholic People: Their Beliefs, Practices, and Values* (Garden City, New York: Doubleday, 1987), 51; William D'Antonio, James Davidson, Dean Hoge, and Ruth Wallace, *American Catholic Laity in a Changing Church* (Kansas City, Missouri: Sheed and Ward, 1989), ch. 4; Archbishop Quinn spoke of the widespread opposition to the encyclical's teaching at the 1980 Synod on the Family; see his "New Context for Contraception Teaching," *Origins* 10 (1980) 263-267.

[13] Thomas J. Reese, "2001 and Beyond: Preparing the Church for the Next Millennium," *America* 176 (1997) 12.

of Catholic baby boomers say that the development of Church teaching ought to be in the hands of the hierarchy and laity, not in the hands of the hierarchy alone."[14]

A new phenomenon is the number of Catholics who, putting personal needs ahead of ecclesial loyalty, join other churches. Literally millions of Hispanic Catholics have left the Catholic Church in recent years for Evangelical and Pentecostal congregations. In the U.S. alone, Andrew Greeley estimates that in the last quarter century the equivalent of one out of seven Hispanics has left the Catholic Church, and almost half of Hispanic Protestants belong to moderate or liberal Protestant denominations.[15] Furthermore, this ecclesial mobility is not limited to Hispanics. Many Protestant seminaries and divinity schools have a number of formerly Catholic women preparing for ordination in their churches. In one evangelical seminary with which I am familiar, three of the last student body presidents have been former Catholics.

What this in effect means is that the contemporary Catholic Church has to a considerable extent lost its ability to define the religious good for its members, and thus to control their lives and religious practice. For many the Church is no longer seen as an institution embodying salvation for those submissive to its authority, but as a sign of salvation in a world from which God is not absent. Church affiliation and practice is seen as voluntary rather than obligatory.

At the same time, in the United States a growing conservative movement skillfully exploits the differences between the bishops, trying to hold together a diverse and pluralistic church, and Rome.[16] Ultra conservatives attack progressive bishops in their publications, often providing the address of Roman curial officials and encouraging their readers to write directly with their complaints. Some have gone to Rome in the battle against the U.S. bishops' efforts to introduce a moderate inclusive language lectionary, with consider-

---

[14] Roof, *A Generation of Seekers*, 234.

[15] Andrew M. Greeley, "Defections Among Hispanics (Updated)," *America* 177 (1997) 12.

[16] See for example Archbishop Rembert Weakland, O.S.B., "Liturgical Renewal: Two Latin Rites," *America* 176 (1997) 12-15.

able success. A group of new Catholic apologists, many of them converts from Protestantism, are popularizing a polemical apologetics that has much in common with Protestant fundamentalism. Their work appeals to many Catholics today who, concerned or even frightened by the direction of contemporary Catholic theology and life, welcome what they consider an "orthodox" presentation of their faith, even if it means a return to a defensive, fortress Catholicism. There is indeed a separatist dimension to the new apologists' critique. As Peter Huff of Saint Anselm College observes, "Like dissident theologians engaged in 'internal emigration' and women-church feminists proposing a temporary 'space apart' from patriarchal church and culture, the new apologists locate authentic Catholicism in the diaspora, not the promised land of the National Council of Catholic Bishops or the U.S. Catholic Conference."[17]

Many of the bishops are frustrated; they feel that they cannot bring issues they want to discuss to the table and have been at times prevented from developing their own answers to crucial pastoral issues, as for example, the U.S. bishops voting in 1992 to abandon their attempt to develop a pastoral letter on women, after repeated Roman interventions. Pastors and priests find themselves caught between a hierarchy they cannot influence and a people they can no longer command. Many refrain from preaching on disputed issues such as the Church's sexual ethics; they seek instead to encourage others to live lives of faith, nourished by prayer and the Scriptures.

How can the Catholic Church remain a community united in faith and mission? Some advocate an uncompromising adherence to what they understand as the received tradition; they try to maintain in the face of contrary evidence that church teaching does not change, that what is needed is not dialogue but clear and authoritative teaching, that all the answers to contemporary questions can be found in the new *Catechism of the Catholic Church*, that those who don't agree should leave. But such an approach is neither wise nor catholic.

---

[17] Huff, "New Apologists in America's Catholic Subculture," *Horizons* 23 (1996) 256.

The late Cardinal Joseph Bernardin's "Common Ground" initiative was an attempt to deal with the growing polarization that so often characterizes internal Catholic debates; he wrote: "A mood of suspicion and acrimony hangs over many of those most active in the church's life; at moments it even seems to have infiltrated the ranks of bishops."[18] His initiative, proposed practically from his death bed, was criticized by four of the U.S. cardinals, while a fifth took issue with Archbishop Quinn's Oxford address.[19]

The church today is confronted by many difficult questions which need honest discussion, among them, the shortage of priests and the right of communities to the Eucharist, a more collegial style of church leadership, allowing the laity some participation in its decision-making processes and the formulation of its teaching, addressing the special concerns of women, minorities, the divorced, and those in mixed marriages, renewing its ethical teaching particularly in the area of sexuality, and allowing for greater adaptation and inculturation at local levels and in different cultures. These are challenges as great as any in the church's history, and they arise, not out of a modern secular spirit, but precisely out of those currents of renewal unleashed by the Second Vatican Council.

If, as Archbishop Quinn says, Catholics today have a new consciousness of their baptismal dignity and of their own responsibility for the mission of the church, and in a culture which places a high value on experience, self-determination, participation, and the acceptance of difference, the church needs to find ways to exercise authority in a more collegial and inclusive way, to face issues honestly, to build consensus.

At the same time, there is among other Christians a growing recognition of the need for a Petrine ministry of unity, but those who express this are quick to add that this ministry must be reformed. The papacy as it is presently exercised remains an obstacle to unity. This is the "new situation" that the church faces. It calls for the reform of structures, not just to carry out the commitment

---

[18] Joseph Cardinal Bernardin, "Called to be Catholic: Church in a Time of Peril" *Origins* 26 (1996) 167.

[19] See the excellent response by Bishop Kenneth E. Untener, "How Bishops Talk," *America* 175 (1996) 9-15.

to Christian unity reaffirmed by Pope John Paul II in *Ut Unum Sint*, but also to maintain its own unity and catholicity as a community of faith. With this in mind, let us move to consider the reform of structures that the archbishop suggests.

THE REFORM OF STRUCTURES

Quinn states that to ask about new ways of exercising the primacy that is "open to a new situation" is to raise the question of the reform of the papacy (7). He begins by proposing a structural reform of the curia, to be carried out by a special commission with a three member presidency and working commission members from the bishops, priests, religious, and laity (11-12). He suggests that the bishops of the Church are being hindered from exercising their threefold role of sanctifying, governing, and teaching in a fully collegial way by the interposing of administrative structures such as the curia or the papal nuncios between the pope and the rest of the episcopate (12-13). He gives numerous examples, of decisions being made in Rome by Vatican congregations which override the decisions of episcopal conferences, of important issues facing the Church which the bishops are not free to discuss, of an unwillingness to allow greater diversity on pastoral and liturgical issues, of episcopal conferences and local churches having little say in the appointment of bishops.

Others have made similar criticisms. Cardinal Godfried Danneels, Archbishop of Mechelen-Brussels, raised many of the same points in a call for greater consultation between pope and bishops in a 1997 interview.[20] Francis Sullivan notes that the Congregation for the Doctrine of the Faith failed to consult the International Theological Commission, a commission of eminent theologians established by Pope Paul VI, in formulating at least three of its documents, *Mysterium Ecclesiae* (1973), *Persona Humana* (1975), and *Inter Insigniores* (1977), the last named its controversial statement on the inadmissibility of women to the priesthood.[21]

---

[20] Godfried Danneels, interview published in *Origins* 27 (1997) 339-341.

[21] Francis A. Sullivan, "Authority in an Ecclesiology of Communion," *New Theology Review* 10/3 (1997) 27-28.

Among Quinn's suggested reforms I would single out the following.

1. The Synod of Bishops

Arguing that the procedures of the international synod of bishops
are outdated, Quinn suggests that the synod would become more
truly collegial if it were given a deliberative rather than merely a
consultative vote (18).

There has been some controversy over whether the acts of the
synod are truly collegial acts of the episcopal college. Patrick
Granfield agrees with those who maintain that they are collective ·
acts rather than strictly collegial ones, since only the entire *ordo
episcoporum* can be the subject of a collegial act. And he sees this
position as supported by the Code of Canon Law which describes
the synod as an advisory body.[22] It should not be conceived as a kind
of ecclesiastical parliament, with elected representatives.

Thus the archbishop's suggestion goes beyond how present canon
law understands the synod. Still, it is not impossible. The new Code
(1983) places its canons on the synod after its treatment of the
Roman Pontiff and the college of bishops and before those dealing
with the cardinals, the Roman curia, and the papal legates. Though
the synod's role is consultative rather than deliberative, the Code
recognizes that the pope can in some cases give the synod deliberative power; in these cases he must still ratify its decisions (c. 343).
There are also a number of steps that might be taken to enable the
synod to function in a more collegial manner.[23]

First, the bishops ought to be able to have more say about what
questions appear on the synod's agenda. While it is important for
the pope to be able to bring his concerns to the synod, it is equally
true that the bishops should be able to raise for discussion those

---

[22] Patrick Granfield, *The Limits of the Papacy: Authority and Autonomy in the
Church* (New York: Crossroad, 1987), 91-92.

[23] See Granfield, *The Limits of the Papacy,* 92-97; Thomas P. Rausch, "The Synod
of Bishops: Improving the Synod Process," *The Jurist* 49 (1989) 248-257; Thomas
J. Reese, *Inside the Vatican: The Politics and Organization of the Catholic Church*
(Cambridge, Massachusetts: Harvard University Press, 1996) 60-65.

issues which they see as affecting the good of the church. At present, their ability to do so is very limited. The synod secretariat consults with the episcopal conferences in regard to themes and topics to be treated in the *lineamenta* or outline, to which the conferences then submit responses. But the pope is free to ignore all their recommendations in choosing a topic.[24]

The synod provides the Church with a permanent structure to enable it to address the issues with which it is confronted. If the bishops were to insist that a particular issue appear on the agenda, the issue would have to be faced. But an exaggerated sense of loyalty to the pope frequently inhibits them from raising difficult questions. Thus as Quinn notes, "issues of major concern in the church are not really open to a free and collegial evaluation and discussion by bishops. . . . In subtle ways and sometimes in very direct ways, the position of the curia on these issues is communicated to bishops at synods and intimidates them" (17).

Secondly, the rule of secrecy needs to be relaxed. It is true that the secrecy that surrounds the preparatory phase and the actual debates at the synod sometimes might enable those from episcopal conferences in countries where the church experiences persecution to speak more freely. Yet too often what one of the lay auditors at the 1987 synod called a "wall of secrecy" still surrounds the synod process.[25] As Granfield has pointed out, excessive secrecy can give the impression that the debate is not open and that the bishops are not accountable to the wider church.[26]

Third, the synod reporting process needs to be revised. The problem here is that the synod process resembles a funnel which filters the diversity of opinions expressed on the floor down to an acceptable common denominator. But that means that minority views which represent the needs of particular episcopal conferences or local churches do not always get passed on to the pope in the recommendations. The problem is compounded when the editorial committee doing the filtering is not composed of members of the

---

[24] Reese, *Inside the Vatican*, 48.

[25] Dolores R. Leckey, "The Synod of '87: A View from the Aurelian Wall," *America* 158 (1988) 208.

[26] Granfield, *The Limits of the Papacy*, 93.

synod itself, but of conservative advisors appointed by the Vatican, as was the case at the 1987 Synod on the Laity. Here, where four members of the editorial committee were members of Opus Dei, a number of specific proposals which found considerable support on the floor—for example, admitting women to those liturgical ministries not requiring ordination—were formulated in so general a way in the final list of propositions presented to the bishops for their vote that they were no longer specifically mentioned. As a result, the bishops were not able to express their opinion on the issues originally raised.

There is also considerable frustration over the gap which so often exists between the issues presented at a synod and the official response that follows. According to James Dallen, the papal position in the apostolic exhortation following the 1983 Synod on Reconciliation "differs in either content or style from the statements made in the synod and from the direction suggested by the report on the confidential propositions given him by the Synod" on social sin, general absolution, and alienated groups within the Church.[27] Passing minority reports along to the pope or recommending the establishment of commissions to study the concerns of particular churches would improve the synod process considerably.

Fourth, the membership of the synods should be expanded. Though the Synod is precisely a synod of bishops, canon law allows for the election of a determined number of nonepiscopal members from clerical religious institutes (c. 346) and others have attended as nonvoting members. At the Synod on the Laity in 1987 there were twenty theological experts and sixty lay auditors who participated with the bishops in the small discussion groups. Providing in this way for a broader membership allows for some participation of the laity in the church's decision-making process. The synod remains the only structure which provides a forum where bishops, theologians, and representatives of the religious orders and laity from all over the world can come together to share their views on important issues and make recommendations to the pope. The episcopal conferences should be consulted in naming these nonepis-

---

[27] James Dallen, "*Reconciliatio et Paenitentia*: The Postsynodal Apostolic Exhortation," *Worship* 59 (1985) 100.

copal participants, whether theological advisors or lay auditors; they should not simply be appointed by the Vatican. Also reducing the number of members from the Roman curia would make possible greater representation from local churches.[28]

Fifth, the time between synod meetings should be increased. A longer period than the present three years is needed for preparation. Episcopal conferences which generally meet only once or twice a year need more time to study issues and respond to the lineamenta. It has been suggested that the synod meet every four years.

Finally, as we saw above, the pope can endow the synod on occasion with deliberative power. In such a case, its authority would remain that of a synod, rather than of the entire episcopal college.[29] Still, allowing the synod to function occasionally as a deliberative body would be a sign of the church's determination to move toward a more truly collegial style of decision-making. Even if the church is not ready to take this step, the pope cannot ignore what clearly emerges as the judgment of a synod. Its resolutions can carry at least a moral authority to which the pope needs to give serious consideration.

2. Calling a Council

Another suggestion of the archbishop is that the church might call a council to mark the beginning of the new millennium. He is not the only one to make such a suggestion; a number of church leaders and theologians have proposed that the beginning of the third millennium would be a fitting time to summon a council of the whole Christian church. Quinn's concern is to recapture the importance of councils in the life of the Catholic Church, perhaps with regularly scheduled meetings (18).

Although the Catholic Church might profit from a council, in my own judgment the time is not yet ripe. At the present time, over two-thirds of the Church's bishops have been appointed under the present pope's administration. As Thomas Reese has written:

---

[28] Reese, *Inside the Vatican*, 64.

[29] See Charles M. Murphy, "Collegiality: An Essay Toward Better Understanding," *Theological Studies* 46 (1985) 42.

The Vatican is using the litmus test of birth control, priestly celibacy and women's ordination (and liberation theology in Latin America) to screen the undesirable and disloyal from consideration as candidates for the episcopate. Vocal defenders of papal positions are promoted even if they are unpopular with their people and the other bishops.[30]

Even granting that the views of many originally conservative bishops evolve as a result of their pastoral experience, a more systematic approach to ecclesial renewal should begin with a renewal of the episcopacy. Indeed, that is one of Quinn's major points. It is a crucial one.

3. The Appointment of Bishops

Quinn notes that as late as 1829, only 24 of the 646 diocesan bishops in the Church were directly appointed by Rome, and that the present system was much influenced by political conditions in nineteenth century Europe (21). But this was a response to a particular problem, contrary to the general tradition of the church which recognized the right of local churches to select their own bishops. Pope Celestine I (422-432) declared: "Let a bishop not be imposed upon the people whom they do not want."[31] Pope Leo I (440-461) stated: "He who has to preside over all must be elected by all."[32] In 1305 Pope Clement V tried to reserve the right of appointing bishops to himself, but bishops continued to be chosen by local authorities, sometimes kings, sometimes cathedral clergy. One factor behind the rise of the all powerful, monarchical papacy in the nineteenth century was dissatisfaction with bishops chosen by kings and queens.[33]

Perhaps no issue today is more important than that of the appointment of bishops. Quinn recognizes that there are some advantages to the present system which can safeguard the process from local pressures and state interference, but he rightly urges that local

---

[30] Reese, "2001 and Beyond," 14.

[31] Jacques-Paul Migne, editor, *Patrologia Cursus Completus, Series Latina.* 221 Volumes (Paris: Garnier, 1844-94) 50:434.

[32] Jacques-Paul Migne, 54:634.

[33] See Costigan, "Papal Supremacy," 15-16.

churches "have a significant and truly substantive role in the appointment of bishops" which should include a meaningful role for priests, laypersons, and religious (21).

Canon law recognizes the possibility of local churches choosing their own bishops: it states that the pope "freely appoints bishops or confirms those lawfully elected" (c. 375). Thus a renewal of the process of episcopal appointment would grant to local churches the right to name their own bishops, or at least to present a *terna* (list of three candidates) to Rome. The crucial issue for church unity is not Roman appointment but recognition by the Apostolic See, so that a bishop selected locally and his church are in communion with the universal church.

4. Subsidiarity and the Reform of Canon Law

Archbishop Quinn places considerable emphasis on honoring the principle of subsidiarity in the Church's exercise of authority, observing that it is linked with the doctrinal truth of collegiality. He points out that both Pius XII and the Preface to the 1983 Code of Canon Law stated explicitly that the principle of subsidiarity applies to the inner life of the Church (22).

Yet it is not so clear that the Church has fully embraced the applicability of the principle to its own life. As Ad Leys, a former staff member of the Dutch Bishops' Conference has argued, there is some ambiguity on this point in the tradition. In spite of Pius XII's statements on the applicability of the principle, it was not applied to the Church itself in the constitutions and decrees of Vatican II.[34] The 1983 Code referred to it in its Preface, but Leys argues that there is no evidence of a deeper understanding of the validity and consequences of the principle in church law.[35] Indeed, he maintains that the 1983 Code seems to accentuate the primacy even more than the 1917 Code did. For example, though Vatican II used the term "vicar of Christ" of bishops as well as pope, the new Code uses it only of the pope. Canon 333.2 says that the pope is

---

[34] Ad Leys, *Ecclesiological Impacts of the Principle of Subsidiarity*, trans. A. van Santwoord (Kampen: Kok, 1995), 89.

[35] Leys, *Ecclesiological Impacts*, 99.

always in communion with the other bishops, but has the right to exercise his office of supreme pastor in either a personal or collegial manner. Leys concludes, "In effect, the Code of 1983 opens all the doors to a centralist exercise of primacy."[36]

Thus it should not be surprising that the 1985 Extraordinary Synod, referring to Pius XII, recommended "that a study be made to examine whether the principle of subsidiarity in use in human society can be applied to the church and to what degree and in what sense such an application can and should be made."[37]

At the end of his study, done in response to the synod's challenge, Leys argues that what he calls the "tensile relationships" which constitute the church as a *communio*—that is, the relations between pope and bishops, universal church and particular churches, as well as church and individual believers—must be more clearly defined than they are in the present Code.[38] Though he does not specifically call for a reform of the Code, his study clearly implies that one is needed to safeguard these tensile relationships.

CONCLUSIONS

In the final section of his address Archbishop Quinn contrasts two different approaches to church government, one political, the other ecclesial: "The fundamental concern of the political model is order and therefore control. The fundamental concern of the ecclesial model is communion and therefore discernment in faith of the diversity of the gifts and works of the Spirit" (26).

The reforms he suggests represent an effort to restore a proper balance between order and discernment, one that seeks in the Spirit to find God's will for the church. To put it simply, he is asking that bishops be allowed to exercise a "true, active collegiality and not merely a passive collegiality" (16), and that the principle of subsidiarity be honored in church administration. This is not to ask for the impossible. While it involves a reform of the way authority is

---

[36] Leys, *Ecclesiological Impacts*, 100.
[37] The Extraordinary Synod of Bishops, *The Final Report*, Origins 15 (1985) 449.
[38] Leys, *Ecclesiological Impacts*, 209-210.

exercised, it could be accomplished within the present prescriptions of church law.

Canon law already recognizes the possibility of synods of bishops exercising on occasion deliberative power or of local churches selecting their own bishops. Allowing bishops and episcopal conferences to exercise an active collegiality by seeking their advice and consent on doctrinal, liturgical, and disciplinary questions and honoring subsidiarity by enabling them to make pastoral decisions on issues facing their churches depends only on how the primacy is understood and exercised.

However the present Code needs to be updated in order to give better juridical specification to the cooperation that ought to exist between the primacy and the college of bishops, as well as to safeguard the rights of individual Christians, as Ad Leys' study suggests.

In his 1996 visit to Germany Pope John Paul emphasized that "evangelization and ecumenism are indissolubly linked" and he stressed that the "task of evangelization equally concerns all Christians—Catholic, Orthodox and Protestant."[39] It is this concern for evangelization, so typical of this pope, that he returns to at the end of his encyclical on ecumenism, *Ut Unum Sint*. He reaffirms that the lack of unity among Christians contradicts the truth of the Gospel (no. 98) and exhorts all to follow the promptings of the Spirit toward full and visible unity (no. 99).

The new situation he sees at the beginning of the third millennium may be the kairotic moment for reform, not just for the well-being of the Catholic Church itself, but also for the Christian unity that so many desire. Hopefully, it is not too late. Many, perhaps discouraged by the enormous task of changing institutions, are beginning to speak of a new kind of ecumenism, a "new paradigm" which stresses local collaboration, working together for justice and peace, and manifesting the unity already given rather than striving for visible unity of churches.[40]

---

[39] John Paul II, "Linking Evangelization and Ecumenism," *Origins* 26 (1996) 140.

[40] See Konrad Raiser, *Ecumenism in Transition: A Paradigm Shift in the Ecumenical Movement?* (Geneva: World Council of Churches, 1991).

The most radical structural reform Quinn calls for has to do with the Roman curia, to be carried out by a special commission with a broad representation of different constituencies in the Church. This would be an important Roman initiative toward the reform so many desire. It remains to be seen if Rome will be willing to take this step.

"Searching for God's Will Together": A Response to Archbishop Quinn

Wendy M. Wright

Creighton University

At the conclusion of his wonderfully loving and forthright address "The Exercise of the Primacy," delivered at Oxford in June of 1996, Archbishop John R. Quinn uttered these heartfelt words:

> My reflections . . . are offered as a response to the pope by one who wishes to walk with him in an unbreakable communion of faith and love on the costly journey of discovery as together we search for the will of God (28).[1]

It is precisely at this point of convergence—the communal search for the will of God—that this modest response to the Archbishop's words will be located. Discernment is the art that concerns itself with this search. And the spiritual tradition, both as a cumulatively lived practice in the church's history and as a theoretical discipline, is in great part about discernment. Considered from the viewpoint of this tradition, the Oxford address raises complex yet pressing issues. This response will be two-fold. First, against the backdrop of what Quinn describes as the political and ecclesial models opera-

---

[1] Parenthetical citations refer to pages in Archbishop Quinn's lecture as printed in this volume.

tive in the church today, I will reflect upon the historical tradition of discernment, alluding especially to the lives and witness of those among us whom we have raised up as saints.[2] What does the tradition of discernment teach us about being church? In other words, who discerns, what is the process of discernment and how do we best discern together? I will suggest that these insights pertain not only to the exercise of the primacy but to all members of the church body. Second, taking my cue from the Archbishop who, in his turn echoing John Paul II, locates his Oxford words in the context of the "new situation" in which the church finds itself today (4-5), I will speak to the "new situation" in regard to the tradition of Christian spirituality.

THE TRADITION OF SPIRITUAL DISCERNMENT

The Oxford address is primarily concerned with what Quinn sees as the discrepancy between Pope John Paul II's expressed desire to discover new forms of the papal ministry suited to the contemporary ecumenical climate and the pope's failure to practice the genuine collegiality with the bishops that has been at the heart of the church's life from early times and which would ease ecumenical relations. Instead, the pope has exercised what Quinn terms "collaboration," a form of leadership that has (a) relied upon the bishops primarily as consultants on an agenda that has already been predetermined, (b) restricted serious consideration of questions deemed "closed," (c) placed a curial bureaucracy between the bishop of Rome and his fellow bishops, and (d) overruled the carefully deliberated teaching actions of a conference of colleagues (13, 14-15).

Collaboration rather than collegiality seems to be a feature of a church that values order and control above all else. At the conclu-

---

[2] This notion of the saints as the pioneers in each era who make the inexhaustible fount of Christ's holiness visible comes from Karl Rahner, S.J. See his *Theological Investigations* III, *The Theology of the Spiritual Life* (Baltimore: Helicon Press, 1961), 91-104. Further, William M. Thompson in his *Fire and Light: The Saints and Theology: On Consulting the Saints, Mystics and Martyrs in Theology* (Mahwah, New Jersey: Paulist Press, 1987) argues convincingly that these luminaries are an essential source for our communal theological reflection.

sion of his statement Quinn makes allusion to the two models of church at work in the church today, the political and the ecclesial (26). Quoting St. Bernard's admonition to Pope Eugene III that he seemed more the successor of Constantine than Peter, Quinn states:

> Bernard's comment readily brings to mind the tension between the political and the ecclesial model at work in the church. The fundamental concern of the political model is order and therefore control. The fundamental concern of the ecclesial model is communion and therefore discernment in faith of the diversity of gifts and works in the Spirit. The claims of discernment and the claims of order must always coexist for one cannot be embraced and the other rejected. They must always exist in tension. But it is always wrong when the claims of discernment are all but eliminated in favor of the claims of order thereby making control and the political model the supreme good (27).

The Archbishop's comments are well taken and, while agreeing with him that the need for order in the church is an ever-present reality, against the backdrop of the historic traditions of Christian spirituality, I will speak to the questions of discernment and the necessary cultivation of an ecclesial rather than a political model of church .[3]

What is at stake here is the question of discernment in the entire church. The Oxford address's poignant concluding appeal to "together . . . search for the will of God" (28) is not merely rhetorical. Discernment of God's will, or sensitivity to the prompting of the living divine Spirit is the central and, perhaps, the only truly

---

[3] What we today call "Christian spirituality" has gone under a number of names and described a variety of phenomena over the centuries. Sometimes it has been known as a branch of practical theology—i.e. ascetical and mystical theology—sometimes it has been construed solely as the interior life of prayer, sometimes it has been identified with ascetic, vowed lifestyles, sometimes as the reception of dramatic charismata or gifts. In all cases, at the core, the Christian spiritual tradition has, as its name suggests, been about the Spirit, about the attentive, responsive, cooperative harkening to the Spirit's movements. Put another way (although the very rephrasing in English may put something of a different cast to it), it is about the discernment of God's will.

necessary function of the church as a living body. It is a project in which each of us is intimately engaged.

In terms of the bishop of Rome and his fellow bishops, Quinn is firm in his reminder that such discernment has never traditionally been conceived as a discernment done solely from one source. It has been, rather, a shared undertaking. He makes reference to the principal of "subsidiarity" that Pius XII enunciated as a principle operative for the Church as well as secular society: "[A] larger social body with more resources does not routinely absorb the role or functions of smaller and less powerful bodies. But it does help and support the smaller bodies to be able to fulfill their own role" (22).

This principle is illuminating when applied to the practice of discernment. It is suggestive of St. Paul's vision of the church in I Corinthians 12 as an organic unity in which a variety of gifts are bestowed by the Spirit for the full and fruitful life of the body. From this perspective, discernment is a matter of sharing and sifting and weighing the gifts by the ripeness of their fruits. This oversimplifies Paul, but the image is a useful one.

This analogy is not only useful in the case of pope and bishops. In the same manner, discernment should take place at all levels of the church: in individuals, in families, among small faith communities, in parishes, in the diocese.

There has been a marked tendency at various points of the church's history, including the present pontificate, to assume that discernment and obedience to authority are the same thing, to assume that the Spirit's promptings are always and unerringly felt at the tip of the pyramid of the structure, at whatever level, be it a pope among his bishops, a bishop among his priests, an abbot among his fellow monks, a pastor among his congregation, or a father in his family. (I would note parenthetically that all of those traditional pyramid perchers are male). An opposing extreme tendency would be to assume that the Spirit's promptings are received randomly and atomistically, that whatever an individual experiences as revelatory of the will of God must necessarily be such.

A more balanced and traditional view would thread its way between these two extreme tendencies. Discernment is not best seen as obedience to authority nor as spiritual anarchy. In this regard, St. Francis de Sales, deemed by us Doctor of the Church, is wonderfully illuminating.

De Sales postulated that, since God (in God's essence) is beyond human comprehension, knowledge of God's "will" in its fullness is not available to any of us. Nevertheless, we human beings have access to what he referred to as the "two wills of God"—two modalities through which we get glimpses of the divine wisdom that shapes the world. The first of these modalities deSales called "the signified will of God." This will was known through all the ordinary means by which we have learned to practice discernment. We pray, we pore over scripture, we listen to the teachings of the church through its doctrine, its practice, its ministers, its saints, we consult trusted spiritual advisors and the words of eminent thinkers, we attend to the stirrings of conscience. Then, having sifted and weighed all our considerations through the sieve of the texture and weight of the desire of our own hearts, we arrive at a sense of the next step, the direction to turn, the action to follow. The fruits of this very human activity, de Sales affirms, must be accepted as the "signified will of God" and we should act upon it vigorously.

There is however, according to the seventeenth century saint, another modality that makes God's will known to us. De Sales calls this the "will of God's good pleasure." This is encountered in the situations and events of life that seem quite outside our control—those political, social, economic, environmental, familial, psycho-biological, and institutional realities in which we are immersed. These too can be expressions of "God's will"—the "will of God's good pleasure."

The point here is *not* that we make earnest discernments using our own efforts and come up with what we think is God's will and then discover that the real will is locatable in the fixed circumstances in which we find ourselves. Nor is it the case that fixed circumstances are never the "real" will, but that our personal discernments always clearly mediate divine intentionality. Instead, de Sales teaches us to live and move between the two wills of God with boldness and freedom. We must work vigorously on behalf of what we glean to be the "signified will." Yet we must be willing to abandon our discernment if the "will of God's good pleasure" intervenes. It is in the creative tension *between* agency and abandonment that true fidelity lies. Clearly, for de Sales, discernment is neither unreflective submission nor following some predetermined formula, nor simply following one's own whims. Rather it is a way of walking in the world, open to the Spirit as manifested in the concrete reality of everyday life.[4]

Francis de Sales was not addressing the papacy, the episcopacy, or an ecumenical audience when he considered the two wills of God. But he was convinced that discernment was a spiritual art form for all the church. He believed that the Spirit in his own era was enlivening men and women in all ranks and states in life—green-grocers, housewives, soldiers, and bishops—"devout souls" who together were engaged in the creative work of letting "Jesus live" in the world. At the heart of that work was the practice of discernment.[5] The Genevan bishop reminds us that the Spirit's movements are felt solely neither from the bottom nor the top, the inner nor the outer realms. Certainly, priority must be given to promptings that carry the weight of tradition and community, for these represent the church's cumulative wisdom but that weight must never be used to crush or control but rather as balance in the delicate tension held between the "signified will" and the "will of God's good pleasure."

This crucial art of discernment must be exercised in the church today, not only in the arena in which the world's bishops and the

---

[4] For a discussion of "Living Between the Two Wills of God" see *Francis de Sales and Jane de Chantal: Letters of Spiritual Direction*, translated by Peronne Marie Thibert, V.H.M., selected and introduced by Wendy M. Wright and Joseph F. Power, O.F.S.F. (Mahwah, New Jersey: Paulist Press, 1988). The analysis is based primarily on his *Treatise on the Love of God*, books VIII and IX.

[5] There are some limits to citing saints as timeless authorities, for some of what they say has atrophied due to the limitations of the view they formed in their specific historical context. De Sales, for example, is not always particularly helpful on questions of social justice for a twentieth century church with its century-old articulated tradition of social teaching, which critiques the social and economic structures that impoverish and oppress classes of people, since he assumed with his contemporaries that wealth and poverty, aristocracy and peasantry were states in life somehow fixed by the divine order. Nevertheless, with such reservations, de Sales can be a wonderfully typical and balanced teacher of discernment.

bishop of Rome attune themselves to the Spirit's promptings, but in all parts of the Body. Archbishop Quinn's moving plea that brings closure to the Oxford address underscores this point:

> Christ as Lord makes everything new, a new heaven, a new earth, a new humanity. He is drawing us all forward into the future by the Spirit of this new covenant of love. We and the whole of creation are straining toward that future that God has prepared for those who love Him and do His will (27-28).

It is not the pope or bishops alone who are thus straining. Each of us, created in God's image as we are, discovers this deep straining forward at the substrata of our being. How we respond together to that straining is fundamental to the dawning of the new heaven and earth. And the response must happen in all parts of the Body. A telling illustrative example of how this can occur can be seen in the arena of the family—the domestic church. The example is fitting not only because John Paul II has turned our collective attention toward the family and its role in the creation of the civilization of love, but because the domestic church is an authentic church in and of itself.[6] It is a primal unit of church, a community of mutual need and nourishment that struggles to look upon and act toward one another as God's children, and to extend that gift to the wider world. The family is a "sacramental" reality in that it makes visible in the form of shared communion and mutual forgiveness, the hidden ground of love that sustains us all. Much more than simply a tiny subdivision of the parish church or the mere recipient of the teaching, preaching, healing, and reconciling of the gathered church's efforts, the domestic church is an authentic community of discernment.

Some models of Catholic family life would see spiritual discernment within the domestic church much in the same way that the present pope sometimes appears to practice discernment within the context of the episcopate. It mirrors Quinn's political model. The prompting of the Spirit are in this model mainly the prerogative of the father with wife and children becoming recipients of the dis-

---

[6] See John Paul II, "The Christian Family is a Vocation to Love," *L'Osservatore Romano*, English edition, 6 January 1993.

cerned wisdom of the father. Even if this model is modified some-what to allow for some participation of wife and children, a basi-cally pyramidal version of discernment may prevail. The weakness of such a model for attending to God's will is that it identifies persons with their social roles rather than with the charisms or gifts that they possess. Further, it spiritually impoverishes those in the family not in positions of authority. It assumes that God does not and cannot work through all of the beloved sons and daughters who were created in the divine image.

The opposite extreme of familial spiritual anarchy is not necessar-ily the only alternative to this pyramidal model. Another and viable vision of family discernment, one attuned to Francis de Sales' teachings, would see husband and wife as engaged in a delicate process of mutual discernment, a carefully shared process of listen-ing to the "signified will" as it emerges from both of them individu-ally as well from their shared concerns. Children would enter into the process as they mature, gradually accepting more responsibility for the discernments in family as they develop. The exercise of authority in the family would thus be a shared activity, with parents sharing the burden as the children are growing. Their exercise of that authority would never be for its own sake but for the gradual empowerment of their children who, in their own turn, would grow into such exercise. In terms of discernment, the family would thus be training its youth to grow into their rightful freedom as children of God, a freedom to be part of the delicate and mutual process of discerning God's will together.

This family model of mutual discernment, which mirrors Arch-bishop Quinn's ecclesial model (26-27), suggests that, while different roles are played within the body and different gifts are offered and received, discernment cannot be assumed to be the sole prerogative of any one person or group. Discernment is something we do together. Nor is it unthinkable that the clearest articulation of God's will might emerge from the little ones among us—the children in the family, the laity or families in the church. Insistently the spiri-tual tradition has affirmed that promptings of the Spirit can and do emerge among the littlest and the least as well as among the elite, that genuinely inspired words are not the prerogative of those in

positions of power and authority.[7] Conversely, it must be remem-
bered that there are mature adults in all parts of the body—among
clergy, laity, bishops, parents, religious women, people in the

[7] For example, consider the cases of St. Juliana of Liège and of St. Margaret Mary
Alacoque, both obscure religious who were the recipients of visions that urged the
establishment of public observances, the Feasts of Corpus Christi and the Sacred
Heart, that in fact became universally recognized on the church calendar. There
are clearly an entire cluster of factors that enabled these two otherwise anony-
mous women's spiritual experiences to gain public validity, but the point is that
the tradition of spirituality has always given a preference to the "little tradition"
as a privileged locus for the Spirit's activity. History bears this out as a continuing
preference. Francis and Clare of Assisi in the thirteenth century baptized material
and spiritual poverty as the hallowed place of divine encounter. Thérèse of Lisieux
gave us her "little way." The Latin American church of the twentieth century has
given us the "option for the poor." It would be a mistake to see these variations on
an ancient theme as simply a series of aberrations. Rather, they might be seen as
a persistent intuition that the Spirit has a preference for the little and the lowly.
We should bear this in mind when we seek together to discern the will of God.
    An image from St. Catherine of Siena comes to mind here. This remarkable
woman, another Doctor of the Church, painted a word picture of the church as
a vast vineyard in which each of us has our own discrete vineyard. Yet none of the
separate plots, while they remain distinctive, is fenced off from the other.

> You then, are my workers. You have come from me, the supreme eternal
> gardener, and I have engrafted you onto the vine by making myself one with
> you.
>   Keep in mind that each of you has your own vineyard. But every one is
> joined to your neighbors' vineyards without any dividing lines. They are so
> joined together, in fact, that you cannot do good or evil for yourself without
> doing the same for your neighbors.
>   All of you together make up one common vineyard, the whole Christian
> assembly, and you are all united in the vineyard of the mystic body of holy
> Church from which you draw your life. In this vineyard is planted the vine,
> which is my only-begotten Son, into whom you must be engrafted (*The
> Dialogue*, translated by Suzanne Noffke, O.P. [Mahwah, New Jersey.: Paulist
> Press, 1980] 62).

Catherine's vision of radical, organic interconnectedness accords well with her
experience of the movement of the Spirit. She, a reputedly illiterate Italian
laywoman, a Third Order Dominican, advisor of popes, spiritual guide to a band
of devoted followers, mediator amidst the quarrels of Italian civic politics, was
well acquainted with the fact that the Spirit can enliven anyone, that the Spirit's
movement can be felt in any part of the Body, and that such enlivening is meant
for the comfort, illumination and vitality of the whole.

pulpits and in the pews. All may claim a share in the title "God's children." But as mutual practitioners of spiritual discernment, they may also claim the adult title, "God's friends."[8]

The cumulative tradition of Christian spirituality has taken seriously the reality that God's Spirit moves among us. We must all, popes and bishops, pastors and people, parents and children, women and men, make it our business to search together for God's will. In our searching, let us, to use St. Francis de Sales' words, "live courageously between the one will of God and the other." Both vigorous in our agency and willing in our abandonment, let us genuinely listen to one another, unafraid to raise questions, trusting that the whole Body is truly the Body of Christ, each in his or her own arena exercising the kind of leadership that respects the freedom of the children of God, and let the Bishop of Rome by exercising true collegiality with the world's bishops, model our shared search for the will of God.

We are taught to pray for the Spirit's presence. We have prayed it for centuries in the Pentecost Sequence. We have prayed, together for years, the traditional prayer that is engraved deeply in the hearts of generations of the faithful: "Come, Holy Spirit, fill the hearts of your faithful, and kindle in them the fire of your love. Send forth you Spirit and they shall be created, and you will renew the face of the earth."[9]

THE NEW SITUATION

Archbishop Quinn in his Oxford address situates us within the "new situation" in which the exercise of the primacy takes place. Quoting John Paul II, he underscores how necessary it is for the "forms" of church life to respond to the changing context of each era in history so that the enduring truths of faith might manifest themselves. Quinn especially emphasizes the ecumenically sensitive moment in which we find ourselves (3-5, 7).

---

[8] For a discussion of mutual discernment see my *Sacred Dwelling: A Spirituality of Family Life*, 2nd edition (Leavenworth, Kansas: Forest of Peace, 1994) 87-88.

[9] *Worship: A Hymnal and Service Book for Roman Catholics* (Chicago: GIA Publications, 1963), 1200.

This "new situation" is critical, not only for the continuation of healthy dialogue among representatives of Christian denominations, but for all in the Christian community seeking to discern God's will. What is the shape and texture of this "new situation"? Discernment does not take place in a cultural vacuum, just as the exercise of the papacy does not. Even more significantly, the process of discernment itself is shaped in response to the changing times. The assumptions and parameters of the discernment process, while they remain in continuity with past practice, are modified and reconfigured in each era.

That this is not some smartingly novel occurrence is attested to by the vast variety of documents that emerge from the history of our tradition. Compare, for instance, the classic second century martyrdom of Saints Perpetua and Felicity and the brief seventeenth century treatise, *Abandonment to Divine Providence*, written by Pierre de Caussade, Jesuit confessor to a community of enclosed French Visitandine nuns. The account of the martyrs reveals discernment to be identified with the dramatic charismatic outpouring of the Spirit in an era that was thought to be the final age, bringing about the transformation of the cosmos. In contrast, for the devout community the French Jesuit directed, discernment was a matter of joyfully accepting the "will of God" as it was manifest not only in the ordinary events of life but in the particular, fixed circumstances of that life, the assumption being that those circumstances were divinely foreordained. [10]

Today's practice of discernment likewise takes place in a distinctive context. Two major trends are worth noting. First, the profoundly ecumenical and interfaith practice of the spiritual life today. Second, the falling away of categories that distinguish between

[10] The two young second century North African Christians' names echo around the globe each Easter vigil when churches everywhere solemnly intone the Litany of Saints. They and their cohorts dreamt dreams and saw visions, they foresaw the future, their intercessory prayers freed the dead from their sufferings and reconciled warring factions of the church. De Caussade was writing in a climate in which one's "state of life"—be one aristocratic, peasant, housewife or soldier, greengrocer or "religious" through the maneuverings of one's family—was somehow all ordered in God's place. The difference in assumptions about the nature and practice of discernment in these two eras of the church's history is clear.

groups of people and aspects of reality—laity and clergy, men and women, body and spirit, Christian and non-Christian, rich and poor—which has shaken up dearly held notions about how the Spirit operates.

In the contemporary world, ecumenism consists not simply in a series of official dialogues between leaders of Christian denominations. It is very much a lived reality, especially in the practice of Christian spirituality. In the mid-century that tradition could have been said to be the preserve of the Catholic churches—Roman Catholicism, Eastern Orthodoxy, and Anglicanism—and to be defined by the practice and theory that emerged from Catholic religious, especially, monastic history.[11] In the past several decades, the practice of Christian spirituality has virtually erased denominational borders. Protestant denominations (with the exception of some conservative enclaves) began the process of reclaiming what they have come to see as their legitimate heritage, tracing Presbyterian and Methodist and Baptist approaches to the divine through the post-apostolic centuries, integrating updated traditional spiritual practices such as Centering Prayer, icon gazing, Ignatian meditation, and Prayer of the Heart into their individual and congregational lives. This reclamation, of course, parallels the tremendous resurgence of interest in spirituality in Roman Catholicism itself, a process which gained momentum and focus during Vatican II.

This resurgence has many aspects.[12] Perhaps its most striking feature is its ecumenical nature. Archbishop Quinn addressed himself to an ecumenical audience at Oxford. He spoke about the

---

[11] Thomas Merton was an articulate contemplative spokesman for that world as were his more apostolic contemporaries Dorothy Day and Catherine de Hueck Doherty.

[12] An astonishing amount of scholarly activity, at very sophisticated levels in many academic disciplines, has been generated toward the retrieval, critical editing, translation, and interpretation of classic texts of the historical Christian spiritual tradition. In addition, the current volume of writing in more accessible form about the lives, works and pithy wisdom of generations of saints, holy women, and spiritual masterworks, is almost overwhelming. Spiritual renewal movements abound, houses of prayer crop up everywhere, the practice of spiritual direction is widespread. Some of these developments are denominationally sponsored. Many more are not. Almost all of them are profoundly ecumenical in character.

challenge issued by Pope John Paul II to seek new forms of ministry germane to the new situation. And he quoted the pontiff's own words:

> Could not the real and imperfect communion existing between us persuade church leaders and their theologians to engage with me in a patient and fraternal dialogue in which, leaving useless controversies behind, we could listen to one another, keeping before us only the will of Christ and his church . . . ? (3).

That for which the pontiff and the Archbishop plead is already a reality in the practice of Christian spirituality.

A case in point is the contemporary practice of spiritual direction. Not long ago a spiritual discipline associated primarily with Catholic religious, especially those in community life, spiritual direction has burgeoned. A recent survey from Spiritual Directors International reports a professional membership, while still dominated by Catholics, that is of mixed denominations.[13]

Of even more significance is the fact that spiritual direction is practiced and taught across denominational lines. Presbyterian pastors are guided by Roman Catholic nuns. Catholic laypersons learn the art of icon gazing from Orthodox teachers. Methodists learn lessons in discernment from Quakers. Mennonites are initiated into the world of the Ignatian Spiritual Exercises by Jesuit confreres. In this milieu the practice of spiritual discernment, of knowing God's will, while deeply anchored in the bedrock of Christian tradition, has become unmoored from its denominational specificity. Christians of all stripes and at all levels of church leadership have begun to see the entire interdenominational heritage as legitimately their own.[14]

---

[13] Of an active membership of almost 3,000 from thirty-six countries worldwide, approximately half are Roman Catholic, about 200 are Anglican or Episcopalian, almost 500 are mainline Protestant, the rest are Evangelical, non-denominational, from historic peace churches or are members of religious traditions outside the Christian communion. For these statistics see *Connections* July, 1997 (published by Spiritual Directors International, Burlingame, California).

[14] While this perception may be less common among Roman Catholics, nonetheless it is a rare Catholic in today's pluralistic, intermarried, ecumenically-friendly

Significantly, spiritual discernment is no longer something inexorably linked to denominational polity. In this climate, the political model of church, in which control and order from above is paramount, is a less viable option than the ecclesial model in which genuine mutual discernment is possible. If Episcopalians, Methodists, Roman Catholics, Disciples of Christ and Lutherans can work alongside each other in programs that train spiritual directors nationwide, it is clear that God's Spirit moves authentically in the various expressions of Christianity. To put it concretely: to a present day Catholic participating in a Quaker-inspired clearness committee, a practice which affirms that the Spirit dwells with egalitarian elegance in the hearts of all the gathered listeners, it may begin to seem quaintly anachronistic that the present pope appears to be clutching Peter's keys closer and closer to his chest so that genuine discernment in the Roman Church has become reduced to listening, not to the heart, not to the wider and deeper tradition, not to the voices of trusted advisors, not even to scripture as it unfolds in its historically grounded uniqueness, but to the voice of Rome alone.

What can be said about the ecumenical character of Christian spirituality today is only the tip of the iceberg. To perhaps a lesser degree, but also significantly, the practice of Christian spirituality has been influenced by the interfaith and non-specified religiosity of today's modern world. As an example of how interfaith contact has impacted Roman Catholic perception, one has only to look to the late Thomas Merton and to the compatriots who survived him and continue in monastic vocations.[15] Although the great cross-cultural advances in intermonastic dialogue have quite recently been criticized in Rome,[16] nonetheless, spiritual practices from Buddhist, Hindu, and Muslim traditions have been thoroughly integrated into

environment who would take seriously the idea that journal writing might be inappropriate because it was a favored spiritual practice of American Puritans.

[15] Merton did not go on his final Asian journey as a spiritual tourist but as one who was discovering that the most significant and illuminating interfaith dialogue went on, not in the arena of doctrinal controversy, but in the arena of contemplative praxis.

[16] See *Bulletin of Monastic Interreligious Dialogue* 1996, 1997 (Trappist, Kentucky: Abbey of Gethsemani).

contemporary Christian contemplative theory and practice. Silence, this integrated vision claims, is the most eloquent echo of the divine voice. The same truth is claimed by many non-monastic Christians who, to one degree or another, have sat at the feet of master spiritual teachers from other faiths and have found their own Christian practice there enhanced. On occasion, syncretisms like these are superficial. More often, they are indicative of authentic movements toward spiritual maturity and are grounded in attentive discernment.

A further observation on the "new situation" in which the search for the will of God continues today might be prompted by a visit to almost any large bookstore in America. In the spirituality section one would find an astonishing array of titles. Alongside translations of Teresa of Avila's *Interior Castle* and a CD recording of Hildegard of Bingen's *Hymns and Sequences*, one would find classics from the literature of Taoism, Sufism, Zen and Vedanta, rituals from Native American religious culture, accounts of near death experiences, self-help books that espouse the power of positive thinking, wholistic health advice, pop-psychology pieces that advocate talking to one's inner child, recording one's dreams, or consulting the ancient myths of world cultures to interpret one's inner life. Some of it has enormous integrity, on some the verdict has yet to be weighed in. But it is a dazzling panoply, a textual yardstick of the aching urgency with which the contemporary world longs to both deepen and transcend itself. In this potpourri of offerings gathered under the rubric of spirituality, the gems of wisdom from the Christian spiritual tradition are but one small portion.

The inherent danger, in terms of spiritual significance, is that any one of these gems, derived from either Christianity or from Taoism or depth psychology or whatever, will lose its integrity and efficacy when plucked utterly free from the matrix of theory and practice in which it originated.[17] The equally troubling risk, and this is the

---

[17] Like the recreational use of the Native American sweat lodge by those who are not immersed in the life of the tribe, the free-floating practice of a Christian prayer, say, the Jesus prayer, divorced from the support of a community that celebrates the power and centrality of that name, might run the risk of becoming "recreational" spiritual practice.

one to which Archbishop Quinn alludes, is that committed Catholic
Christians, firmly anchored in their ecclesial moorings, will find
themselves under the precarious leadership of a captain that threatens to dash the Church's precious cargo upon the rocks because it
has anchored itself in too narrow an inlet of papal prerogative, too
small a space for the large dynamic ship of living discernment that
the church has become.

The Oxford lecture makes further reference to the "new situation"
by observing that there are new conceptualizations of the role of
women and the laity abroad today (4). From the perspective of
Christian spirituality, these observations are crucial. The church,
through its spiritual practice, if not always through its doctrinal
articulation or its ecclesial practice, has pointed to the essential
dignity of all persons, men and women, lay and clerical, poor and
wealthy, landed or laborer. Any one of us has always been a potential bearer of the Spirit's message for the entire community. But it
was not until Vatican II and the promulgation of the Universal Call
to Holiness in its *Dogmatic Constitution on the Church* that this long-
implied teaching was given the impetus to flower in the Roman
communion. No longer could holiness be the sole prerogative of
the cloistered or the ordained. Despite the fact that Vatican II's
documents still favor religious vows and priesthood as specially
suited to the cultivation of sanctity, the "people in the pews" have
taken the notion of the Universal Call to Holiness with utter
seriousness. While there certainly are lay persons who continue to
defer to those in religious vows as possessing a superior spirituality
or who would see the distinct spirituality of lay life as separate from
clerical life in both kind and function, for many people, the distinc-
tions between the "states in life" have been washed away. Rather
than expressing itself in a specific lifestyle or role, holiness is construed in the contemporary church as a quality of heart and the
exercise of virtues in whatever lifestyle one finds oneself.[18]

---

[18] One can have a "call" to minister as a visiting nurse or a "call" to care tenderly
for one's own children and aging parents, or one can discover a "call" to exercise
Christian conscience within the legal profession or a "call" to leave the legal
profession and seek work as a youth minister within the church.

The implications of this shift in perspective are significant. The medieval notion that particular states in life and roles within the church carry with them specific spiritual status no longer obtains. More significantly, no longer are specific roles necessarily required of persons determined by their gender, age, and social position. This universal call to holiness invites laity, religious, clerics, women, men, parents, church workers, and those in secular professions to take up the task of discerning God's will. This, as has been suggested, is a task that is best not carried out in isolation but in a reverent attitude of responsive listening to the wisdom of tradition in all its expressions, including the essential leadership exercised by the papacy.

Nonetheless, anyone practicing discernment in their own lives, anyone groping hesitantly yet boldly to test the texture and weight of the spirit's insistent tug on us, will know that this discernment is not a passive act, that the exercise of genuine faith does not consist, like an oarsman in a scull, in simply mechanically heeding orders shouted at one from the prow of the boat. Discernment requires responsible risk-taking, an active engagement with doubt, the boldness and humility to simultaneously trust one's own deepest intuitions and at the same time the willingness to let them go. Discernment means listening for the voice of God which may reveal itself in the rush of the papal whirlwind, the thunder clap of theological formulation or perhaps the whispered cry of the most ignored and forgotten among us.

Archbishop Quinn, through the respectful and forthright words of his Oxford address, invites all of us in the church to engage in a mutual "search for the will of God." That search, conducted with reverence for the traditions which have shaped us, including the traditions of spiritual discernment, and yet in light of the ecumenical and interfaith pluralism of today's "new situation," must be carried out collegially at all levels of the church, between bishops and the pope, between bishops and their priests, between pastors and their congregations, between members of the domestic church. Such a search is ill served by persons who make order and control the primary objectives of our life together. It is better served by those who place the mutual search for God's will at the center of our shared life. Our mutual discernment will not resemble the work of a detective who alone seeks to decipher the secret code that unlocks a preordained divine plan or the work of the cataloguer whose task is to order reality by dropping evidence into neatly arranged files marked "truth" and "not true." Instead, discernment will require us to stand closely together with boldness yet with absolute humility at the tension between what Francis de Sales called the two wills of God.

Response

Most Reverend John R. Quinn
Archdiocese of San Francisco

My Oxford lecture was a Catholic Bishop's attempt to sketch out an answer to the question courageously raised by Pope John Paul II in his encyclical *Ut Unum Sint*: How can the papal office be exercised in a more effective way in response to the new situation among Christians?[1]

I am grateful if my effort has been a service to the pope and to Christian unity. I am honored that it should be so seriously examined by the American Academy of Religion during its national convention. And I am grateful to the five scholars who have commented on my lecture.

My response to the five papers will touch on what appear to me to be one or two more salient points in each, since time does not permit an exhaustive response to everything that has been raised by the individual scholars.

Thomas Rausch makes the point, often raised by others, that the Church is not a democracy and rightly adds that it is not an absolute monarchy either. Yet there is more anxiety expressed about democracy in the Church than about the manifestations of monarchy in the Church. There is here an element of paradox, since the College of Cardinals in its election procedures for choosing the pope is one of the oldest democratic bodies and processes in the world. Democracy is indeed present in the Church at this level. And yet there is

---

[1] See Pope John Paul II, *Ut Unum Sint* (Vatican City: Libreria Editrice Vaticana, 1995) § 95.

a persistent and powerful tendency to read primacy in terms of absolute monarchy. This is interesting because Pope John Paul II himself frequently speaks of collegiality, and in the encyclical *Ut Unum Sint* he explicitly locates the papal office in the context of the Episcopal College:

> When the Catholic Church affirms that the office of the Bishop of Rome corresponds to the will of Christ, she does not separate this office from the mission entrusted to the whole body of Bishops, who are also "vicars and ambassadors of Christ." The Bishop of Rome is a member of the "College," and the Bishops are his brothers in the ministry.[2]

It is also interesting that in this statement, Pope John Paul II does not express all the caveats expressed in *Lumen Gentium* about the College of Bishops: for instance, that it can only act "with Peter and under Peter," that it can only act "with the Head and never without the Head."[3] It is as if this pope has become comfortable with the theology of collegiality and does not find it necessary to express every time what the Catholic Church knows and believes: that the College of Bishops, since it includes the pope and he is its head, must be always in communion and concert with him.

I purposely did not use the word "democracy" in my lecture, fearing that it would be wrongly seized on as an attack on the primacy and that it would deflect attention from the substance and sources of what I said. In this connection I have noticed that, for the most part, those who have criticized the Oxford lecture have not dealt with the sources on which I based my position.

Cardinal Suenens long ago pointed out that democracy and monarchy are both present in some sense in the church but that these concepts cannot be appropriated in the church without certain adaptations. It is not so much whether the church is a democracy as whether the idea of democracy is understood within the framework of Revelation and of the sources of Revelation. Certainly the

---

[2] Pope John Paul II, §95.

[3] Second Vatican Council, *Dogmatic Constitution on the Church*, November 21, 1964 § 22.

Sacrament of Baptism creates a discipleship of equals; yet the Apostolic structure of the church and the Sacrament of Holy Orders constitute a society in which not all have the same function. The Sacrament of Holy Orders cannot simply be collapsed into the Sacrament of Baptism. The church is not a secular, political society and so cannot without qualification be called a democracy. Yet the sources of Revelation clearly show that the church does indeed have some democratic factors. These observations are not directed to the position taken in Fr. Rausch's paper, but to those who use the statement "The Church is not a democracy" as a sort of thoughtless, unexamined slogan calculated to defend an uncritical ideal of a strictly monarchical papacy.

Pope John Paul II, then, shows that he understands the theology of collegiality, and that the papal office is not an absolute monarchy outside and above the church and beyond any claims by the church.

The problem, then, is not at the level of theological understanding but, as I tried to emphasize in the Oxford lecture, at the level of policy and exercise of the papal office. If bishops are described as "brothers in the ministry" and the pope is described as a member of the "College," this is not only a doctrinal statement, it is also programmatic. This truth must be reflected in the way both the pope and the bishops carry out their apostolic office in the church, in the way they see themselves, and in the way they relate to each other. It wounds this understanding of collegiality and brotherly communion when, for instance, the recent document on lay ministries was composed and promulgated without prior knowledge of the episcopate. Several Episcopal Conferences in Europe have made public criticisms of some weaknesses of the document. All this would not have happened if there had been real input by the world's bishops on the proposed text before it was finalized. So far as I can see, most bishops agree that there are abuses. Most agree that the priesthood is not just one among many various other ministries. Most agree that Baptism and Holy Orders are not the same thing. But they do not approach the involvement of lay persons in ministries with fear, but with gratitude and admiration. The concerns of Rome could have been well expressed alongside a more positive approach to the issue.

This repeated mode of procedure, as well as the not infrequent rejection by the curia of decisions made by Episcopal Conferences, is injurious not only to the collegiality of "brothers in the ministry," but to ecumenism as well. It does clearly reflect a strictly monarchical conception of the papacy, strongly favored by the minority element at the Second Vatican Council and all too evidently still favored by important elements in the curia.

The minority in the Council, about three hundred bishops, vigorously opposed the idea of collegiality because they understood the word as it was used in classical Roman law—a body of equals who in turn might delegate one of their number to perform certain functions—and feared it would diminish a monarchical papacy.

The majority of the Council—some 1850 bishops from all over the world—favored and voted for the call for greater collegiality of pope and bishops but, while they acknowledged the unique role of the Successor of Peter and his prerogatives, they did not locate the papal office outside the College of Bishops and consequently did not understand the papal office as standing by itself without any reference to the episcopate or the church.

A second point made by Thomas Rausch is that a "growing neoconservative movement skillfully exploits the differences between bishops . . . ."[4] This interesting observation reveals the general confusion abroad today between orthodoxy and integralism.

Integralism is not true orthodoxy. True orthodoxy knows that the church grows in its understanding and in its expression of the faith. True orthodoxy knows that not everything is a matter of faith. Integralism admits no changes and, worse, no growth. It stifles the Spirit, deifies the past, and lives, not in hope, but in perpetual fear. Both Pope John XXIII and Pope John Paul II gave expression to this distinction between orthodoxy and integralism. The New Catholic Encyclopedia states forthrightly:

> Integralism was intellectually and tactically dangerous to the Church.
> It threatened to substitute routine for genuine tradition and to hamper
> the development of Catholic thought by refusing to disengage living
> traditions from attitudes or procedures dictated by the needs of the

---

[4] Thomas P. Rausch, S.J., "Archbishop Quinn's Challenge," 76, above.

moment. With their connections in high ecclesiastical circles the integralists attempted to safeguard Catholics by enclosing them in a ghetto inaccessible to the outside world, where a few would make all decisions and the mass of the faithful would do no more than comply with them.[5]

Both Pope John XXIII and Pope John Paul II gave expression to this distinction between orthodoxy and integralism. John XXIII, when in the opening address to the Council he declared that, "The substance of the ancient doctrine of the deposit of faith is one thing, and the way in which it is presented is another." John Paul II, when in *Ut Unum Sint* he explicitly reiterates the words of John XXIII (§ 81) and then makes a similar distinction about the papal office: " . . . I have a particular responsibility . . . in heeding the request made of me to find a way of exercising the primacy which, while in no way renouncing what is essential to its mission, is nonetheless open to a new situation." (§ 95) Both popes distinguish in doctrine the substance and the manner of expression and John Paul II, in the area of ecclesial structure, distinguishes between the substance of the papal office and the forms, style, and manner of its exercise. Both popes admit that there can be change, that there must be change, and call for change.

But it would be illusory to think that either kind of change could take place without profound reflection and probing, and therefore without new insights which place both in new perspective and thus bring about true doctrinal development so odious to integralism.

Scott Appleby likens the present situation in the Church to the situation at the beginning of this century. It would be difficult to fault this comparison especially if one has read Gerald Fogarty's excellent work on the relationship of the American bishops and Rome at the end of the last century and the beginning of this century. Appleby describes this as "the enclave culture and the integralist mentality."[6] Its results in the early part of the century he

---

[5] "Integralism," *s.v., New Catholic Encyclopedia* (New York: McGraw-Hill, 1967) VII:552. N.B.: The imprimatur for this volume of the Encyclopedia was given by Cardinal Patrick O'Boyle, of Washington, D.C.

[6] R. Scott Appleby, "Ending As It Began?" 32, above.

describes as "debilitating consequences" leading to "a fractured and fractious faith community."[7]

One of Appleby's significant observations, which he cites from Gerald Fogarty, is that "Integrism in the American Church took place not through the repression of scholarship . . . but through the gradual Romanization of the American hierarchy."[8] For me, there is an important truth here. Does it mean simply that bishops who have been students in Rome especially in their formative seminary years are all of one mold? I think not. For example, men as different in outlook as Francis Cardinal Stafford and Hans Küng both did their seminary studies in the same Gregorian University. Nor does it mean that bishops who did all their studies in the United States are not Romanized.

But just what does "Romanization" mean? It can mean, of course, the Catholic belief that "all the churches must be in communion with this church," as Irenaeus said. This is a doctrinal stance. It means a deeply internalized sense of Rome as the center of communion and as the guardian of legitimate diversity.

But it can mean a veneer of Roman ways and usages. For example, some, after leaving Rome, cultivate curial ways of speaking, certain curial formalities, the diplomatic politesse that conceals through clever, even witty, discourse while always alert to obtain information. For some it is a form of narcotic that puts to sleep all critical judgment and sets aside even the most classical theological principles governing the interpretation of Roman documents and Magisterial teaching.

True Romanization, as I see it, is the discovery of the great tradition of the church and, above all, the rediscovery of Rome's first title in the earliest written tribute to her, the church "who presides in love." True Romanization is the living sense of the catholicity of the church down the centuries of manifold cultures and circumstance; the greatness of her saints and martyrs many of whom suffered not only for her but because of her, who loved her and were faithful in her communion unto the end. Unfortunately in some quarters in Rome and elsewhere, Romanization is under-

---

[7] Appleby, 33, above.

[8] Appleby, 38-39, above.

stood only in a dim and narrow way as conformity to only one of many legitimate ways of thinking, and its grandeur and power lost and dissipated.

The pseudo-Romanization described by Appleby is unable to distinguish between fidelity and loyalty. Loyalty is a pliant conformity. Fidelity is Aquinas' saying "I am the friend of Aristotle but a greater friend of truth." Fidelity is never to deny failure, weakness or error. Fidelity has the interior freedom to raise a voice of brotherly correction enjoined by the Gospel itself, but always in that love that is stronger than death and that many waters cannot quench.

John Kane writes that "It is ironic . . . that Archbishop Quinn had to wait until after his retirement to address the topic of the primacy . . . ."[9] The fact is I did not "wait." I resigned in December, 1995. The encyclical was only promulgated in May of 1995. I had never before thought about addressing this specific topic. During the months following its publication I was considering what topic to address at Oxford. A theologian friend of mine suggested this topic. And so it was the encyclical itself, which asked for a response, and the suggestion of a friend, that led me to develop my lecture on that topic. It had not been in my mind prior to this.

Kane might be read to imply that my reference to the "new situation" is my own creation. Actually, it is the pope himself who speaks of the "new situation." Examination of his words in *Ut Unum Sint* make clear that in effect he is saying, "The church is in a new context, a new situation. It has new prospects and new opportunities. And the exercise of the Papal office has to change to meet this new situation."

Kane also touches on the issue of subsidiarity, which I developed in my lecture. Further reflection and conversation with an Orthodox theologian leads me, however, to see it in a larger perspective now than I did a year ago. The Orthodox theologian who brought this to my attention, cautioned me not to think of "subsidiarity" in terms of higher authority conceding something to other authorities in the Church. In a personal letter to me, he wrote:

---

[9] John Kane, "Roman Catholicism and the Contemporary Crisis of Authority," 59, note 4, above.

In effect, subsidiarity means a concession by a central power which delegates certain powers or functions to a subordinate for some practical reason of the moment. But in the case we are dealing with this does not apply. What must be resisted is an inappropriate centralization which, as such, injures the inalienable rights of the bishops and the only way to rectify this is to restore national and provincial councils to their proper place of honor, in keeping with the Council of Trent and the Ecumenical Councils of the first millennium.

Given the doctrine of collegiality, so clearly affirmed by Pope John Paul II, bishops already are true pastors by reason of their ordination. It is significant that the Council teaches that the College of Bishops is created not by a juridical act but by the act of sacramental ordination. It is true that the functioning of the College of Bishops is regulated by canonical authority for the sake of the good order and common good of the church. But the College of Bishops is not created by a juridical act. Bishops, then, by reason of their ordination and in collegial communion, already possess all the authority they need to govern and serve their churches. The Orthodox perspective, rooted in this reality, would understand subsidiarity not as giving the bishops something they do not have but rather as removing any obstacles to their ability to pastor their churches in the name of Christ, in the context of communion with the head and other members of the Episcopal College.

Elizabeth Johnson makes a timely point in her references to Mary Magdalene. I, too, had noted that, as John XXIII and the Council both affirmed, the role of women is among the more prominent signs of our times. Pope John Paul II has also emphasized this theme even addressing an encyclical to the whole church on the topic. But the issue as I see it is not so much at the level of theory or theology as at the level of church practice. Certainly progress has been made. There are women holding important positions in the Roman curia, for instance. But in regard to the curia, more needs to be done. The question must be asked why qualified women could not hold the highest positions in curial offices and congregations. If the curia is the instrumentality of the pope, women could surely be placed at the head of certain departments and congregations such as the

Pontifical Commission for Justice and Peace, the Pontifical Commission for the Family, the Pontifical Commission for the Interpretation of the Code, the Congregation for Catholic Education and various others. The role of women needs much further prominence if the Church is to respond to what the Council and the popes have called one of the important signs of the times.

I would like to add a comment about Professor Johnson's statement, "Quinn's collegial model has strong resonance with the vision of church . . . as a church in the round . . . a community of the discipleship of equals."[10] With the Council I acknowledge that from one point of view, let us say from the point of view of Baptism, the church is indeed a communion of equals. But if the church is the People of God it is also the Body of Christ, in which not all members have the same function and in which no member is dispensable. The Council in deliberating about collegiality was very concerned that it not say anything which would imply a negation of the unique role and prerogatives of the Successor of Peter or which would place the Successor of Peter outside the College of Bishops. The authentic mind of the Council was that while collegiality is to be affirmed, the unique role of the head of the College is also to be affirmed but always seen to be within the College of Bishops.

Wendy Wright brings out what is ultimately the most important point of in the search for Christian unity: the will of God and true spiritual discernment. She writes, "Discernment of God's will . . . sensitivity to the . . . Spirit is the central and, perhaps, the only truly necessary function of the church as a living body."[11]

Yet I just want to add the clarification that in light of this search for the will of God, the church has solemn and specific responsibilities to guard the apostolic deposit, to protect and defend it, to interpret it, to hand it on unadulterated, to guard unity and charity among believers and many other things which should not be overlooked. But Professor Wright is correct in highlighting the paramount importance of the search for the will of God which I focused on at the end of my lecture.

---

[10] Elizabeth A. Johnson, "On Going Fishing," 53, above.

[11] Wendy Wright, "Searching for God's Will Together," 91-92, above.

She introduces the teaching of Francis de Sales on the two wills of God: the will of God as we grasp it after careful efforts to discover it—prayer, counsel, reasoning on the subject—and the will of God as it becomes manifest through circumstance and state in life—the providential signs. While this is without question a helpful approach, in my own reference to the ultimate importance of seeking the will of God in the search for Christian unity, I had in mind Ignatius Loyola's approach. For Ignatius there can be no effective search for the will of God unless the seeker has true indifference. Ignatian indifference is not apathy. It is rather a firm determination and desire to sacrifice everything in order to do the will of God when it becomes clear. The great Jesuit Cardinal, Carlo Martini, called it "interior freedom," freedom of heart that imparts a freedom to do the will of God. The will of God is not always pleasant. It may be very exacting and demand immense sacrifice. Elizabeth Seton, for instance, when she finally understood that God wanted her to be a religious, had to sacrifice her home, her social position, her family. Father Stanley Rother, an American pastor in a Guatemalan village, on advice returned to Oklahoma when he was placed on the death list. But over a period of several months he came to see that it was the will of God that he go back and face death with his people: "The Shepherd can't run away," he said. Doing the will of God led to his death, murdered by the civil authorities like so many of the people of his parish.

So for the Christian churches, if we truly want to seek the will of God in regard to our unity, all of us will have to make great sacrifices. Things cannot just go on the way they are. That is why I pointed out to non-Catholic Christians in my lecture that the first search must be the will of God and that it is not appropriate to wait until each group finds a papacy which perfectly conforms to all human ideas of the perfect. Similarly, the Catholic Church will have to be prepared for sacrifices, and all will have to have that interior freedom and trust in God which Ignatius calls indifference in order to embrace the often hidden and mysterious path of God's will.

This in turn is impossible without serious and prolonged prayer. That is why the ultimate condition for Christian unity will be found in the determination of Christians to pray and to pray with an intensity that is truly contemplative. Karl Rahner has said that in the future Christians will be contemplatives or there will be no Christians. I concur with Professor Wright that the most significant factor in interfaith dialogue is in the arena of contemplation.

Unlike other encyclicals, *Ut Unum Sint* is not addressed to any individual or group of persons. It is an open *cri de cœur* to all. This seminar, its five papers, and my Oxford lecture have all been a serious effort to respond to the question addressed to all of us by Pope John Paul II. The effort to do so has sharpened our perception of some things in the Church which we all believe need to be changed or modified. But as I have reflected on all this, read hundreds of books and articles, and consulted with theologians and other scholars for nearly two years, I have been most struck by the challenge to Catholic faith given by Karl Rahner when he writes:

We do not see the Church so much as the sign "lifted up among the nations," as it was proclaimed at the First Vatican Council. What we now see is the poor Church of sinners, the tent of the pilgrim people of God, pitched in the desert and shaken by all the storms of history, the Church laboriously seeking its way into the future, groping and suffering many internal afflictions, striving over and over again to make sure of its faith; we are aware of a Church of internal tensions and conflicts, we feel burdened in the Church both by the reactionary callousness of the institutional factor and by the reckless modernism that threatens to squander the sacred heritage of faith and to destroy the memory of its historical experience.... Attachment to the Church must be part also of the spirituality of the future. Otherwise it is elitist arrogance and a form of unbelief, failing to grasp the fact that the Holy Word of God has come into the flesh of the world and sanctifies this world by taking on himself the sin of the world and also of the Church.

The ecclesial aspect of the spirituality of the future will be less triumphalist than formerly. But attachment to the Church will also in the future be an absolutely necessary criterion for genuine spirituality.[12]

---

[12] Karl Rahner, *Theological Investigations* 20: *Concern for the Church* (New York: Crossroad, 1981) 152-153.

Afterword

Terrence W. Tilley, University of Dayton
Phyllis Zagano, Boston University

We began our introduction with Pope John Paul II's invitation to church leaders and their theologians to engage with him "in a patient and fraternal dialogue in which, leaving useless controversies behind, we could listen to one another, keeping before us only the will of Christ for his church. . . ."[1] While the dialogue presented in this volume does not include His Holiness, its participants are able, patient and cordial. They focus on key issues and avoid polemic. They both listen to the voices of the others and bring their own insights to the table. They do not seek to open old wounds, obscure embarrassing facts, or forge consensus where none exists. Each seeks to discern, in difficult circumstances, the will of God for the church.

But it is not yet clear how we ought understand the will of God for the church. Pope John Paul II and Archbishop John R. Quinn each highlight the new situation for the exercise of the primacy. The other authors agree and develop their own variations on the theme of the "new situation." Yet the fact that we live in a new situation is not in itself an unprecedented occurrence. Indeed, historical change seems more constant than historical constancy.

The practice of the primacy developed sporadically as situations changed. Each shift in practice and doctrine was marked by controversy over the will of God. Each stage of development, from the

---

[1] John Paul II, *Ut Unum Sint* (Vatican City: Liberia Editrice Vaticana, 1995) 107, §96.

very beginning of the primacy of honor recognized in the second century to the exemplary and powerful spiritual authority exercised by the "traveling papacy" characteristic of Paul VI and John Paul II, is a response to a "new situation." History teaches us that the conflicts between the primate and the episcopate are ongoing. The belief that there ever was a perfect harmony—or that there will be perfect harmony in the church before the eschaton—is unwarranted. History also teaches us that discerning God's will for the church will never be free from controversy and strongly suggests that the view that there can ever be a final, definitive, and effective theological model for the exercise of the primacy is illusory. Discerning God's will for the church is necessarily an ongoing task, never a settled accomplishment. The practice and the doctrine of the primacy will continue to evolve.

One theme that runs through the essays in this book, foreshadowed in the introduction, is the tension between two ecclesiologies. Each of these ecclesiologies carries a model for the exercise of the primacy that is in deep practical conflict with the other. A "communal" (collegial, ecclesial) model of the church is in conflict with a "juridical" (collaborative, political) model of the church. Simply put, the former recognizes that the church is the communion of saints, united in time and eternity by Baptism. The latter sees that the church is an ordered society, guided and ruled by leaders ordained to their duty. It is not that these two views, at their best, are incompatible. Nor can one properly deny the importance of the insights of the other. What differentiates them are their central or focal values.

The difference in focal value is crucial. Various webs of beliefs that constitute a theology of the church may have the same main insights. Each may agree on all the central claims of the other and differ only in peripheral details. The important theological differences between the most thoughtful communal and juridical ecclesiologies may only be in peripheral matters. But webs of theological beliefs are not abstractions suspended eternally in an invisible, intangible ether. They are embodied in history. Even distinct webs of belief that agree on central claims may seem very different because they have different emphases, different focal values, different views of which beliefs are most central. Controversy emerges when theologians disagree about which values are focal, or when they dispute the best way to express those values and beliefs in a given historical situation. In his summary of the issues disputed at Vatican I, Klaus Schatz makes this point eloquently:

> These controversies were not merely about questions of internal Church structure or the traditional struggle between Gallicanism and ultramontanism. Both sides were essentially concerned with the relationship between the Church and liberal notions of freedom: Should the Church, at a time when the world was in turmoil, locate itself primarily beneath the standard of fixed and unchangeable authority, or present itself more as a historical reality also subject to history and even to change and accepting the modern development of liberty as something in accord with the Gospel?
> The attitude of most of the council fathers was primarily shaped by this polarization.[2]

The new situation the council fathers saw was the emergence of the theory and practice of political and religious freedom. For the church as a community and an institution dedicated to spreading the Gospel, the issue was how to situate the church in and on that landscape. The burning question was how the church and its theology was best to be proclaimed in that new situation, and how the church should manifest the Good News to all. As European society had shifted markedly in response to the French Revolution in 1789 and the multiple revolutions of 1848, the Catholic Church had to respond to *that* new situation.

Obviously, Vatican I lifted up a juridical (collaborative, political) model of the church as the best fit in those circumstances. The winning view led to a model of the church not only as an ordered society, but also as a practical fortress of unchangeable authority against whose bastions the forces of hell could not prevail. Many voices have raised significant doubts about the appropriateness of that juridical, monarchical model in our situation. The current

---

[2] Klaus Schatz, *Papal Primacy: From Its Origins to the Present*, trans. John A. Otto and Linda M. Maloney (Collegeville, Minnesota: Liturgical, 1996) 156.

practices of the curia have raised the hackles of some bishops and theologians, including some of those writing in this volume.[3] The current organization and practice of the curia evolved while a juridical model of the church reigned triumphant.

During the papacy of John Paul II, the notion of the basic ecclesiology of the church as a communion has been gaining considerable ground. Dennis Doyle highlights this shift in the following:

> In "The Final Report" of the Extraordinary Synod of 1985, the bishops presented communion ecclesiology as the key to a proper understanding of Vatican II. They called communion "the central and fundamental idea of the council's documents." More recently, Joseph Ratzinger said of communion ecclesiology that "ultimately there is only *one basic* ecclesiology." The World Conference of the Faith and Order Commission of the World Council of Churches held in Santiago de Compostela in August 1993 was devoted to the theme of the Church as communion.[4]

Although Doyle makes the point that there are multiple versions of this vision of the church in our day, "communion ecclesiology"

---

[3] News reports of what some see as curial "interference" or "insensitivity" are not infrequent. For instance, the elevation of Wolfgang Haas from bishop of Chur, Switzerland, to the new archdiocese of Vaduz, Liechtenstein, brought protests not only from laity, but from the Liechtenstein parliament; see "Bishop's Elevation Protested," *National Catholic Reporter* 34/10 (9 January 1998), 11. The responses of some Catholic bishops, priests, and lay ministers to the "Instruction on Certain Questions Regarding the Collaboration of the Non-Ordained Faithful in the Sacred Ministry of the Priest," issued by eight curial ministries simultaneously, were rather negative. Bishop Lehmann of Mainz, Germany, said the instruction reflects a "climate of mistrust for the laity." Fr. James Driscoll suggested that using the instruction's prescriptions on nomenclature for "chaplains" might cost some lay chaplains their jobs; see John L. Allen, Jr., "Rome issues new limits on lay ministry," *National Catholic Reporter* 34/6 (5 December 1997), 14.

[4] Dennis Doyle, "Journet, Congar, and the Roots of Communion Ecclesiology," *Theological Studies* 58 (September 1997), 461. His references are respectively to *Origins* 14 (19 December 1985), 448; *L'Osservatore Romano* (English edition) 17 June 1992, 1; and Thomas F. Best and Günther Gassman, eds., *On the Way to Fuller Koinonia: Official Report of the Fifth World Conference on Faith and Order,* Faith and Order Paper 166 (Geneva: World Council of Churches, 1994).

is becoming the dominant model of the church in Catholic ecclesiology.

How should the primacy, the Petrine ministry, be conceived and exercised in a "communion ecclesiology" in a world profoundly different from that of 1869? How can the curia operate constructively in service to the church understood as a communion? All of the essays in this volume call for the reformation of the exercise of the primacy and at least imply the need for a reformation in the practice of the Church's central administrative offices. In our view, both the theology of the primacy and the way the Vatican implements it are in serious need of reform. The bishop of Rome must again become the primary center of communion in a polycentric church. The curia must work—and be perceived to work—to facilitate communion among the people of God, rather than to work (and be perceived to work) to bring order to the Pope's subjects. Only facile and false nostalgia makes a return to the ancient "primacy of honor," a Petrine ministry devoid of jurisdictional authority or administrative structure, attractive. The image of the papacy as an unchanging, unchangeable authority has been crushed by the millstone of history, and the monarchical papacy crowned at Vatican I is very difficult to reconcile with Vatican II's vision of the church as communion.

The purpose of all this conversation about the work of the church in concert with Peter's successor is not merely ecclesial self-examination. The church exists not for itself, but to bring the Gospel to all the peoples (Matt. 28:19). The real question is how the Petrine ministry can be exercised best in the present situation to fulfill the essential work of the church in mission: evangelization. Patrick Granfield put it this way:

> The papal ministry can offer love, hope, truth, and compassion to people who are longing for a renewed sense of spiritual values. By demonstrating his solidarity with all humanity, the Pope, through his unique role as head of a large, international, and influential religious organization, is able to communicate effectively the saving message of the Gospel.[5]

---

[5] Patrick Granfield, *The Limits of the Papacy: Authority and Autonomy in the*

The focal image of the contemporary papacy perhaps should not be that of the "vicar of Christ" who holds the keys of the kingdom, but that of the "Apostle to the peoples." His discipleship as bishop of Rome, primate of the Western church, and leader of the universal church should be modeled on that of the Apostles most closely associated with the church of Rome, Peter and Paul. The principle of subsidiarity, not as a principle of the delegation of juridical authority but as a principle of the proper ordering of responsibilities in the communion of the people of God, must govern the operations of the curia.

The principle of subsidiarity has its home in the theology of politics. The slogan "all politics is local" expresses an important truth in politics. Similarly, "all evangelization is local." Under the principle of subsidiarity in the church as communion, the curia's service does not flow from the governing authority of the vicar of Christ, but from the apostolic mission of the whole church. Without such a principle of subsidiarity in the political realm, "civil servant" has the same meaning as "civil master." Without such a principle in the ecclesial realm, *servi servorum Dei*—servants of the servants of God—become indistinguishable from God's elite masters over the rest of God's people. In the communion that is God's church, the people of God must be agents of the Gospel, *servi Dei*. The Petrine ministry, including the curia, must empower each local church, distinctive in its cultural context and diverse from other local churches while united in communion with all the other local churches, to carry out God's will in its own location.

We know the central component of God's eternal will for the church: to proclaim, to manifest, and to bring God's grace to all the peoples. The question is how can the Petrine ministry be thought of and practiced today *ut unum sint*—that all may be one. We hope that this dialogue has contributed and will continue to contribute to answering that question.

Church (New York: Crossroad, 1987) 177.

A Note on the Contributors

R. Scott Appleby (Ph.D., University of Chicago) is Associate Professor of History and Director of the Cushwa Center for the Study of American Catholicism at the University of Notre Dame. He is the author of *Church and Age Unite! The Modernist Impulse in American Catholicism*; co-author of *Transforming Parish Ministry: The Changing Roles of Clergy, Laity, and Women Religious*; and co-editor of *Being Right: Conservative Catholics in America*. He is a member of the board of advisors to the Joseph Cardinal Bernardin Center in Chicago, a participant in the Catholic Common Ground Project, and directs a Cushwa Center research project on the history of twentieth Century American Catholicism.

Elizabeth A. Johnson, C.S.J. (Ph.D., Catholic University of America) is Distinguished Professor of Theology at Fordham University. She is the author of numerous scholarly articles and books, including *Consider Jesus, She Who Is*, and *Women, Earth, and Creator Spirit*. Her newest book, *Friends of God and Prophets: A Feminist Reading of the Communion of Saints*, was published this year. She has served as President of the Catholic Theological Society of America, is a member of the Board of Editorial Consultants of *Theological Studies*, and is on the Advisory Committee of the Dogmatics Section of *Concilium*.

John F. Kane (Ph.D., McMaster University) is Professor of Religious Studies at Regis University in Denver. He is the author of *Pluralism and Truth in Religion*, and of numerous articles, essays, and reviews in scholarly journals. He is past co-chair of the Roman Catholic Studies Group of the American Academy of Religion and founding editor of *Leaven*, a bi-monthly magazine for Rocky Mountain region Catholics.

John R. Quinn (S.T.L., Gregorian University, Rome) was ordained priest for the Diocese of San Diego in 1953. He served as Associate Pastor at St. George's Parish, Ontario, California and later as professor of theology at Immaculate Heart Seminary, San Diego. In 1967 he was ordained Auxiliary Bishop of San Diego, and in 1969 became Pastor of St. Therese Parish, San Diego. He also served as Provost of the University of San Diego. In 1972 he became Bishop of Oklahoma City and Tulsa and in 1973, first Archbishop of Oklahoma City. He became Archbishop of San

Francisco in April, 1977, and was elected to a three-year term as President of the National Conference of Catholic Bishops in November, 1977. In December, 1995, he resigned as Archbishop of San Francisco and is currently engaged in giving retreats and writing.

Thomas P. Rausch, S.J. (Ph.D., Duke University) is Professor and chair of Theological Studies at Loyola Marymount University in Los Angeles. His books include *The Roots of the Catholic Tradition*, *The College Student's Introduction to Theology*, and *Catholicism at the Dawn of the Third Millenium*. He serves on the Theological Commission and the Ecumenical Commission for the Archdiocese of Los Angeles, and on the Editorial Commission for *The Tidings*, the archdiocesan newspaper. He co-chairs the Los Angeles Catholic-Evangelical Dialogue, and is a member of the U.S. Catholic/Southern Baptist Conversation.

Terrence W. Tilley (Ph.D., Graduate Theological Union, Berkeley) is Professor and chair of the Department of Religious Studies at the University of Dayton. He is the author of over one hundred articles, essays and reviews in scholarly journals, and of five books in the areas of philosophy of religion, theological methodology, and narrative theology, including *Postmodern Theologies* and *The Wisdom of Religious Commitment*. He serves as President of the College Theology Society and Co-chair of the Roman Catholic Studies Group of the American Academy of Religion.

Wendy M. Wright (Ph.D., University of California at Santa Barbara) is Professor of Theology at Creighton University. She is the author of numerous articles and six books in the history of spirituality, family spirituality, and spiritual direction, including *Bond of Perfection: Jeanne de Chantal and François de Sales* and *Sacred Dwelling: A Spirituality of Family Life*. She regularly serves as a visiting professor in several graduate ministerial programs in both Roman Catholic and Methodist institutions.

Phyllis Zagano (Ph.D., State University of New York, Stony Brook) is Associate Professor in the College of Communication, Adjunct Associate Professor in the School of Theology, and Director of the Institute for Democratic Communication at Boston University. She is the author of multiple essays and reviews in popular and scholarly journals, and of several books, including *Woman to Woman: An Anthology of Women's Spiritualities*, *On Prayer*, and *Ita Ford: Missionary Martyr*. She serves as Co-chair of the Roman Catholic Studies Group of the American Academy of Religion.

Of Related Interest

crossroad
herder